Learn
Chinese
Cooking
in Your
Own Kitchen

Learn Chinese Cooking in Your Own Kitchen

Gloria Bley Miller

Grosset & Dunlap
Publishers   New York
A FILMWAYS COMPANY

❀ FOR R.M.M. ❀

Chinese food is healthful, good-tasting and thrifty. Its traditions go back more than four thousand years, yet are as contemporary as today. The Chinese consume half the meat we do and large quantities of vegetables and grains. Their food is low in calories and highly nutritious.

Some say it's the diet of the future.

FOREWORD

You needn't be Italian to serve lasagna or French to whip up a soufflé. Yet people think you should be Asian to give Chinese cooking a whirl.

Although they often eat in Chinese restaurants, they're convinced the food is too complicated to be cooked at home. They couldn't be more wrong.

Chinese cooking isn't all that mysterious. Some 800 million men, women and children live in China. A goodly number must be cooking what the others are eating. (And what of their relatives who live in the Western world?) If so many people are in on the secret, Chinese cooking can't be much of a mystery, can it?

The real problem is: most people have an "ingredient hangup." They're convinced you can't cook Chinese food unless your cupboard is chock-full of lily buds, shark's fins and quail eggs. Wrong again.

The basic ingredients are meat, poultry, seafood and vegetables, available in any supermarket. Add some soy sauce and sherry and you're well on your way—providing you know how to put it all together.

Consider any style of cooking. You'll find that each is based on how the food is cooked, rather than on the ingredients themselves. And so it is with Chinese cooking. Understanding the method is what it's all about.

The Chinese roast, steam, stew, simmer and deep-fry as others do—with some variations. The only method that's truly unique is stir-frying, which calls for sautéing the ingredients (cut in bite-sized pieces) briefly and rapidly over an intense, but short-lived, fire. Developed centuries ago, stir-frying was a way of coping with fuel shortages then. It still makes sense today.

Master stir-frying and you virtually master Chinese cooking. This book will tell you how. And tell you as well about five other basic cooking techniques with which you can prepare literally thousands of dishes.

Chinese cooking is a great culinary adventure if you just relax and enjoy it. Its methods are so flexible, they can work with just about any ingredient on hand. And you may be as imaginative or creative as you like. Most delightful of all, familiar foods—cooked the Chinese way—take on a beautiful appearance and a great new taste.

GLORIA BLEY MILLER

New York City

PLANNING THE MEAL

A three-pound chicken served at a Western-style dinner, along with a salad, potato and dessert, will feed about four. At a Chinese meal that chicken will serve six to eight.

By the same token, eight ounces of meat, considered sufficient for one or at most two people in the West, will serve four or more Chinese. And the fish that feeds two or three in one style can serve four to six in the other.

This seeming discrepancy is easily explained: The Chinese serve a number of "main" dishes at their meals, rather than only one, as is the Western custom. This adds considerably more interest and variety to the fare. It also creates the illusion that one is eating a greater quantity of food than one actually is.

For example, a Chinese meal for four might include a soup, a stir-fried meat-and-vegetable dish, a fish and a vegetable, along with rice and tea. To serve six, another meat dish and seafood dish would be added. For eight, there would be three meat dishes, two seafood dishes and two vegetable dishes, along with the customary soup, rice and tea.

As a result, the number of servings for a given recipe cannot be given accurately. They always depend on whether the meal is served Chinese or Western style, on the number of diners present and on the number of dishes served.

CONTENTS

❀ *Stir-frying* ❀

ALTHOUGH THE COOKING of China was hardly born yesterday, the Western world has only now begun to understand its true dimensions. Chinese cooking, somewhat belatedly, is being declared the equal of the French. Some say it goes far beyond it.

In any case, the Chinese have been involved with food for more than four thousand years—the peasants concerned mainly with their survival; the emperors and philosophers interested in the aesthetic values as well. Confucius once said that the ideal Chinese gentleman loved not only learning but life; not only refinement but food.

Today the vast and sophisticated cuisine of China encompasses thousands of dishes, yet employs less than a dozen basic techniques. The most special of all is stir-frying—a form of rapid sautéing that quickly blends and harmonizes disparate ingredients. This technique, seldom used in the West, makes possible almost limitless combinations of meats, poultry, seafood and vegetables.

One can better grasp the spirit of stir-frying by discovering the wok, a thin metal cooking pot that looks like a coolie hat with a rounded bottom. The wok's shape, which has remained constant for centuries, was originally determined by the shape of the early Chinese stoves—open cylinders of clay and later brick, fueled by wood or coal, atop which the semispherical pan sat securely. On today's stoves a metal collar is needed to keep the wok from rocking like a ship at sea. All woks—available in Chinese grocery and hardware stores and a number of department stores as well—are sold with these stabilizing collars.

Woks range in diameter from 10 to 32 inches, with the 12- or 14-inch size most suitable for home use. They're made of various metals, most commonly iron * or stainless steel. (An iron wok may not be as elegant as a stainless steel one, but it works just as well.) Wok lids, which often must be purchased separately, are extremely useful to have. Generally made of aluminum, they have sloping sides, a straight flat top and an easy-to-grasp handle. The higher the dome of the lid, the more it increases the wok's capacity—which proves particularly helpful when Chinese cooking methods other than stir-frying are used.

Two other important wok accessories are a spatula to flip the ingredients and a ladle to add or remove cooking liquids. Both are often used simultaneously, one in each hand, to toss the ingredients in a lifting, dropping motion, somewhat in the manner of tossing a salad, then to scoop them up when cooked. The spatula's blade is nonflexible and rimmed on three sides. Its slightly rounded bottom surface slides easily around the curved interior surface of the wok.

As substitutes, an ordinary spatula and standard soup ladle will do. In place of the wok itself, a 12-inch skillet can be used if its sides slope somewhat and it is sufficiently wide and deep to keep the ingredients from scattering all over the stove.

---

* Iron woks must be seasoned to seal up the metal pores so the food won't stick. Here's how it's done: Wash the wok thoroughly with hot water and a detergent, then rinse and dry. Slowly heat two tablespoons of vegetable oil in the pan until the oil seems to move around the bottom. Carefully tilt and rotate the pan until all of its inner surface is coated with oil. Then turn off the heat. Let the wok cool and discard the oil. Wipe the inner surface with paper toweling until smooth and lightly oiled.

Once seasoned, a wok is practically self-cleaning and should never be scoured with strong detergents or metal cleaners. Plain hot water and the flick of a brush are usually sufficient. Food scraps that stick can be scoured off with salt.

The wok, described as the most useful cooking utensil ever devised, is shallow enough for sautéing; deep enough for parboiling, simmering, poaching, steaming and deep-frying. (It also lends itself to such endeavors as crepes and southern fried chicken.) But it is in stir-frying that the wok really shines.

In stir-frying, the ingredients are sliced, diced or shredded, then briefly tossed in a small amount of oil over intensely high heat. The heat quickly seals in both the juices and the nutrients, making meats succulent; helping vegetables retain their color, freshness and texture.

Stir-frying evolved from a civilization buffeted by floods, droughts and famines. The chronic scarcity of food and fuel made it necessary to cook whatever nourishment there was as

quickly as possible. For this the wok's shape and construction were ideal: The thin metal could quickly concentrate the heat from a single small fire, while the smooth curving sides, sloping toward a central well, conducted the heat evenly over the entire surface.

Vitally important is the intensity of the heat that flows up and around the bottom of the wok. Chinese restaurants now have high-powered gas units that generate almost as much heat as a home furnace. (This makes it possible to cook such dishes as Mu Shu Pork or Lobster Cantonese in about two minutes. It takes a few minutes more in home kitchens.)

Gas stoves work best for stir-frying because their flames can be instantaneously raised or lowered. Electric stoves are more of a problem. Flat pans work better with them since direct contact between the heating element and the pot is needed. (To regulate the temperature, the heat should be set to high and the pan slid on and off the burner.)

Although stir-frying may at first seem complex and baffling, it's based on one simple idea: that each ingredient has its own cooking time; that tender foods need less heat and tougher ones need more. Thus, the various ingredients—depending on their cooking requirements—must be added to the pan at different times so that all in the end will be ready at the same time.

Success in stir-frying depends on good advance preparation. This includes cutting, marinating, measuring and mixing. Uniformity in cutting is essential both for appearance and evenness in cooking. If the meat, poultry or seafood is sliced, diced or shredded, so indeed must be the vegetable. The marinating calls for coating the meat, etc. in a seasoned cornstarch mixture—a paste, not a liquid—made variously of cornstarch, sherry, soy sauce, salt, sugar, pepper and unbeaten egg white. This flavors the meat while sealing it in for its first contact with the searing oil. Ingredients for stir-frying can be marinated as briefly as 15 minutes or as long as overnight.

Essential to the preparation is arranging all the ingredients near the stove in the sequence in which they'll go into the pan. Once cooking begins, the tempo accelerates so rapidly that every minute counts. When their time comes, ingredients must be tossed into the pot in split-second succession, then constantly flipped about with a rapid, flicking motion from all directions to the center. Once the fat is literally on the fire, there isn't time to dash about looking for an ingredient, trying to mix a sauce or slice a vegetable.

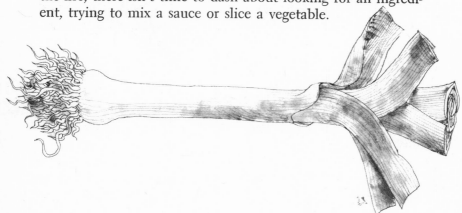

Stir-frying is the antithesis of passive cooking. It calls for a sense of sequence, a sensitivity to the right amount of heat and the right amount of doneness. Yet it offers considerable scope to the imagination. Eventually it becomes a kind of free-wheeling technique done almost intuitively, with a great and liberating sense of exhilaration.

Stir-frying consists of a number of steps whose general pattern follows. However, the sequence is somewhat flexible, since the vegetables may be cooked first and the meat afterward. This is how it's done:

1. Heat a pan over high heat until hot enough to sizzle a drop of water. When dry, add a tablespoon or two of oil. Spread the oil to coat the bottom of the pan, either with the spatula or by rotating the pan itself. Heat the oil until bubbling and easy flowing but not quite smoking. (Peanut or another vegetable oil may be used but not olive oil.)

2. Add and stir in the first seasonings, such as garlic, scallions, fresh ginger root, salt, etc. When the garlic, etc. becomes golden and aromatic, add the meat. Toss and flip it vigorously to prevent burning and assure even cooking. At this point, add no other liquid. (If the meat is still raw, the liquid

will toughen it.) However, if the pan gets too dry, add a little more oil. Never pour this oil directly on the meat but heat it first in a small clearing at the bottom of the pan—made by pushing the food aside—or else add the oil with a wide circular motion inside the rim so that it runs down, and is heated by, the metal sides of the pan.

3. When the hot oil has sealed in the flavor and partly cooked the meat (beef will lose its redness and begin to brown, pork and chicken will lose their pinkness and turn white and shrimp will turn pinkish), add the liquid seasonings, such as soy sauce and sherry. These, used in small quantities, enable the meat to go on cooking at high temperatures without burning while at the same time intensifying the meat's natural flavors. (Although medium-dry sherry is frequently used in place of Chinese wine, sake, brandy or gin may also substitute.) The liquid seasonings are never poured directly on the ingredients. (They might be absorbed and concentrated in one part of the pan.) They, too, are added in the same manner as the additional oil.

4. Remove the partly cooked meat and set it aside. Rinse the pan with hot water and dry. Heat more oil. Add the vegetables a fistful at a time. (This will keep the temperature from dropping too quickly.) Soft vegetables, such as spinach and lettuce, require only a minute or two of cooking, while less tender vegetables need to simmer briefly in a small amount of stock. The stock is heated in the same way as the additional oil and liquid seasonings: either by adding it around the sides or pouring it directly into the well of the pan. The pan is then covered for two or three minutes of additional cooking. Tougher vegetables, such as carrots or string beans, may be parboiled first to shorten their cooking time. (Chinese restaurants do this frequently.)

5. When the vegetables are three-fourths done, the meat is returned to the pan and the ingredients quickly stir-fried until the meat is reheated and the flavors blended. A stir-fried dish is always better dry than wet. If it has generated a lot of liquid, pour off the excess, leaving about half a cup. This liquid or gravy can now be thickened if desired. The ingredi-

ents in the pan are pushed aside, and cornstarch—blended to a paste with cold water—is stirred in over high heat until the gravy thickens slightly. Then the ingredients get another whirl or two and the food is served. Chinese restaurants invariably thicken their pan liquids in this manner. Many home cooks don't thicken them at all.

Note: Should you wish to increase the quantities of a stir-fried dish, you can, but never add more than a pound of meat to the pan at once (the temperature will drop too quickly). And never stir-fry more than two batches for a given dish, since the ingredients will cool down too much beyond that.

An old Chinese proverb asserts that it's better that a man wait for his meal than the meal wait for the man. This is certainly true for stir-frying. The dish should be served the moment it's cooked. Should it linger on the stove a minute or two longer, food that's crisp, delicious and fragrant will quickly lose its color and become soggy and tasteless. Since actual cooking time is brief, the waiting will be negligible. And the lovely aroma that emanates from the kitchen only enhances the anticipation.

Note: Because of variations in individual stoves and cooking pots, it's impossible to standardize the stir-frying time for any Chinese recipe. One must always keep an eye on the food, not on the clock. The hand must be on the stirring, the mind on the next step. All the senses are involved, particularly common sense. If a vegetable starts to scorch, lower the heat at once. If it begins to wilt, take it out of the pan.

STIR-FRIED BEEF AND PEPPERS

½ pound flank steak
1 tablespoon cornstarch
1 tablespoon medium-dry
sherry
½ teaspoon salt
2 teaspoons oil
Pinch of sugar

2 or 3 fresh green peppers
2 slices fresh ginger root
1 scallion
2 tablespoons oil
2 tablespoons oil
Pinch of salt

1. Trim the flank steak of its excess fat. Cut against the grain in ⅛-inch slices, then shred into slivers 1 inch long. Place meat in a small bowl.

2. In a cup combine the cornstarch, sherry, salt and first quantity of oil. Add to beef, tossing to coat. Let stand 30 minutes, turning meat occasionally.

3. Meanwhile cut the green peppers in half, removing and discarding their seeds and membranes. Shred in slivers similar to beef. Separately shred the ginger root and scallion.

4. Heat a wok or skillet. Add the second quantity of oil and heat. Add beef shreds and stir-fry over high heat until they begin to brown. Remove from pan.

5. Rinse pan, then reheat. Heat the last of the oil. Add ginger root and scallions; stir-fry a few times. Then add green peppers, salt and sugar. Stir-fry until peppers begin to soften slightly (about a minute). Return beef, stir-frying to reheat and blend flavors. Serve at once.

STIR-FRIED BEEF AND ASPARAGUS

½ pound flank steak
2 tablespoons soy sauce
1 tablespoon medium-dry
sherry
1½ teaspoons cornstarch
½ teaspoon sugar
¼ teaspoon salt

1 pound fresh asparagus
2 scallions
2 slices fresh ginger root
2 tablespoons oil
¼ teaspoon salt
¼ cup chicken stock
3 tablespoons oil

1. Trim the flank steak of its excess fat; cut against the grain in ¼-inch slices, then in strips 1 by 2 inches. Put meat in a bowl.

2. In a cup, combine the soy sauce, sherry, cornstarch, sugar and salt. Add to beef, tossing to coat. Let stand about 15 minutes, turning meat occasionally.

3. Meanwhile break off and discard the tough asparagus ends. Cut off tips on the diagonal and set aside. Then cut stems diagonally in 1½-inch sections. (If stems are thick, peel first with a vegetable peeler.) Cut white scallion stalks in 1½-inch sections. Shred the ginger root.

4. Heat a wok or skillet. Add the first quantity of oil and heat, then the salt. Add asparagus stems. Stir-fry to coat with oil and heat (1 or 2 minutes). Then add tips. Stir-fry another half minute. Add the stock and heat. Cover pan, reduce heat to medium and cook about 2 minutes more. Remove asparagus and set aside.

5. Rinse pan, then reheat. Add the remaining oil and heat, then add scallion sections and ginger root. Stir-fry a few times. Add beef, stir-frying until it loses its redness and begins to brown.

6. Return asparagus. Continue stir-frying to reheat and blend flavors (about a minute more). Serve at once.

STIR-FRIED BEEF WITH MUSHROOMS AND TOMATO

½ pound flank steak
1 pound fresh mushrooms
1 tomato
Boiling water
2 tablespoons oil
½ teaspoon salt

Dash of pepper
1 teaspoon medium-dry sherry
¼ cup chicken stock
1 tablespoon cornstarch
1 tablespoon soy sauce

2 tablespoons water

1. Trim the flank steak of its excess fat; cut against the grain in ¼-inch-thick slices, then in strips 1 by 2 inches. Slice the mushrooms.

2. Plunge the tomato into the boiling water to cover for 20 seconds. Peel at once and cut in small wedges.

3. Heat a wok or skillet. Add the oil and heat. Add the salt and pepper, then beef. Stir-fry until it loses its redness and begins to brown. Sprinkle meat with the sherry; stir-fry a few times more.

4. Add mushrooms, stir-frying to soften slightly. Then add the stock and heat. Cover pan, reduce heat to medium and cook about 2 minutes more. Meanwhile in a cup blend the cornstarch, soy sauce and water to a paste.

5. Stir in the cornstarch paste over medium-high heat to thicken pan liquids. Add tomato wedges, stir-frying a few times to heat through. Serve at once.

STIR-FRIED BEEF AND BEAN CURD

½ *pound flank steak*	2 *tablespoons oyster sauce*
2 *to 3 cakes of bean curd*	2 *tablespoons soy sauce*
2 *slices fresh ginger root*	1 *tablespoon medium-dry*
2 *scallions*	*sherry*
½ *teaspoon sugar*	2 *tablespoons oil*
1 *teaspoon cornstarch*	½ *teaspoon salt*
1 *tablespoon water*	2 *tablespoons oil*

1. Trim the flank steak of its excess fat; then cut against the grain in slices ¼ inch thick and 2 inches long. Place meat in a bowl.

2. Cut the bean curd in similar slices. Crush the ginger root slightly. Mince the scallions.

3. In a cup, combine the sugar, cornstarch and water. Add to meat, tossing it to coat. In another cup, combine the oyster sauce, soy sauce and sherry.

4. Heat a wok or skillet. Add the first quantity of oil and heat. Add the salt, then ginger root, stir-frying a few times. Add meat, stir-frying until it loses its redness (about 1½ minutes). Add scallions. Stir-fry half a minute more. Remove from pan.

5. Rinse pan, then reheat. Heat the remaining oil. Add bean curd slices, tilting pan to coat with oil. Heat through thoroughly, then add oyster sauce mixture and heat. Return beef and stir-fry gently to reheat and blend flavors. Serve at once.

STIR-FRIED PORK AND CUCUMBERS

½ *pound lean pork*	2 *tablespoons oil*
1 *tablespoon cornstarch*	½ *teaspoon salt*
1 *tablespoon medium-dry sherry*	1 *teaspoon medium-dry sherry*
1 *tablespoon soy sauce*	2 *tablespoons oil*
1 *large or 2 small cucumbers*	*Pinch of salt*
2 *white onions*	*Dash of soy sauce*
1 *garlic clove*	*Pinch of sugar*

¼ *cup chicken stock*

1. Cut the pork in ¾-inch cubes and put in a bowl. In a cup, combine the cornstarch, sherry and soy sauce. Add to pork, tossing to coat. Let stand 15 to 30 minutes, turning meat occasionally.

2. Meanwhile peel the cucumber and cut in half lengthwise. Scoop out seeds with a spoon and discard, then cut cucumber

in bite-sized cubes. Peel and cube the onions. Crush the garlic clove slightly.

3. Heat a wok or skillet. Add the first quantity of oil and heat. Add the salt, then garlic. Brown garlic lightly and discard. Add pork cubes, stir-frying to brown lightly on all sides. Sprinkle with the remaining sherry. Stir-fry a few times more. Remove pork.

4. Rinse pan, then reheat. Add the remaining oil and heat. Add onion cubes, stir-frying to soften slightly. Then add cucumber cubes, stir-frying to coat with oil. In quick succession, add the remaining salt, soy sauce, sugar and stock, continuing to stir-fry.

5. When the liquids come to a boil, return pork and stir in. Cover pan, reduce heat to medium and cook until meat is done and vegetables are still crunchy (about 2 or 3 minutes). Serve at once.

NOTE: Cut into a pork cube to check for doneness. If it's still pink, cook a minute or two longer.

STIR-FRIED PORK AND PEAS

½ pound lean pork
1 pound fresh green peas
Water to cover
1 tablespoon salt
1 tablespoon cornstarch
2 tablespoons chicken stock

½ cup cold chicken stock
2 tablespoons oil
½ teaspoon salt
1 tablespoon medium-dry sherry

1. Dice the pork in ¼-inch cubes. Shell the peas.

2. Bring the water to a boil. Add salt, then peas and parboil until softened but still bright green (about 3 minutes). Meanwhile, in a cup, combine the cornstarch and stock.

3. Heat a wok or skillet. Add the oil and heat. Add diced pork, stir-frying until it loses its pinkness. Sprinkle with the salt and sherry. Stir-fry another minute.

4. Sprinkle with the remaining stock and stir-fry about 2 minutes more. (Sprinkle with more stock or sherry, if necessary, to keep meat from burning.)

5. Restir the cornstarch paste and add to pan with par-boiled peas. Stir in over medium-high heat until liquids thicken (a minute or two more). Serve at once.

STIR-FRIED PORK AND BEAN SPROUTS

½ pound lean pork
1 tablespoon soy sauce
1 tablespoon medium-dry
* sherry*
2 tablespoons cornstarch

¼ teaspoon sugar
½ teaspoon salt
Boiling water
1 pound fresh bean sprouts
2 tablespoons oil

1 teaspoon soy sauce

1. Shred the pork and put in a bowl. In a cup, combine the soy sauce, sherry, cornstarch, sugar and salt, blending well. Add to pork, tossing to coat. Let stand about 15 minutes, turning meat occasionally.

2. Meanwhile pour the boiling water over the bean sprouts to blanch. Drain immediately. Chill under cold running water. Drain again.

3. Heat a wok or skillet. Add the oil and heat. Add pork, stir-frying until it loses its pinkness (about 2 minutes).

4. Add bean sprouts, stir-frying to heat through and blend flavors (about 1½ minutes more). Sprinkle with the remaining soy sauce. Stir-fry a few times more. Serve at once.

STIR-FRIED PORK IN LETTUCE ROLLS

1 *pound pork*	2 *teaspoons soy sauce*
10 *water chestnuts*	*Dash of pepper*
2 *slices fresh ginger root*	1 *head Boston lettuce*
1 *tablespoon medium dry sherry*	1 *tablespoon cornstarch*
½ *teaspoon sugar*	¼ *cup cold chicken stock*
½ *teaspoon salt*	2 *tablespoons oil*
1 *tablespoon medium-dry sherry*	

1. Mince the pork or grind coarsely. Place in a bowl. Mince the water chestnuts and ginger root and add. In a cup, com-

bine the sherry, sugar, salt, soy sauce and pepper. Add to pork mixture. Blend well but do not overwork.

2. Separate the lettuce. Wash the leaves and blot dry. In a cup, blend the cornstarch and stock to a paste.

3. Heat a wok or skillet. Add the oil and heat, then add pork. Stir-fry until meat loses its pinkness. Sprinkle with the sherry and continue stir-frying until pork is cooked through (about 3 minutes). If necessary, add a little more sherry to keep meat from burning.

4. Restir the cornstarch paste. Add to pan, stir-frying until mixture thickens.

5. Spoon 2 tablespoons of the mixture onto each lettuce leaf, then roll up the leaf to enclose it. Serve at once.

STIR-FRIED CHICKEN AND MUSHROOMS

1 *large or 2 small chicken breasts*	10 *water chestnuts*
1 *teaspoon cornstarch*	⅛ *pound fresh snow peas*
1 *teaspoon medium-dry sherry*	1 *or 2 scallions*
	1 *garlic clove*
½ *egg white*	2 *tablespoons oil*
Pinch of salt	½ *teaspoon salt*
Dash of white pepper	2 *tablespoons oil*
½ *pound fresh mushrooms*	2 *teaspoons soy sauce*
	½ *teaspoon sugar*

1. Skin and bone the chicken breasts, trimming off any fat or membrane. Cut in slices ½ by 2 inches. Place in a bowl.

2. In a cup, combine the cornstarch, sherry, egg white, salt and pepper. Add to chicken and toss to coat. Let stand 15 to 30 minutes, turning chicken occasionally.

3. Meanwhile slice the mushrooms and water chestnuts. Break off the snow pea tips, removing their strings. Cut the scallions in 1-inch lengths. Slice the garlic.

4. Heat a wok or skillet. Add the first quantity of oil and heat. Add the remaining salt, then mushrooms and water chestnuts. Stir-fry until mushrooms soften slightly. Add snow peas, stir-frying only to heat through. Remove vegetables.

5. Rinse pan, then reheat. Heat the remaining oil. Add garlic and scallions. Stir-fry to brown lightly. Add chicken. Stir-fry until it loses its pinkness. Add the soy sauce and sugar. Stir-fry to color chicken evenly (about 1½ minutes). Return vegetables and stir-fry a minute more to reheat and blend flavors. Serve at once.

STIR-FRIED CHICKEN AND PINEAPPLE

1 *large or two small chicken breasts*	2 *medium onions*
1 *tablespoon cornstarch*	2 *celery stalks*
1½ *tablespoons medium-dry sherry*	12 *water chestnuts*
1 *teaspoon soy sauce*	4 *slices canned pineapple*
½ *teaspoon salt*	1 *tablespoon oil*
	1 *tablespoon oil*
	2 *tablespoons oil*

4 *tablespoons pineapple juice*

1. Skin and bone the chicken breasts, trimming off any fat or membrane. Then cut in ½-inch cubes. Place in a bowl.

2. In a cup, combine the cornstarch, sherry, soy sauce and salt. Add to chicken and toss to coat. Let stand 15 to 30 minutes, turning chicken occasionally.

3. Meanwhile dice the onions and celery to match the chicken cubes. Slice the water chestnuts. Cut each pineapple slice in six pieces.

4. Heat a wok or skillet. Add the first quantity of oil and heat. Add onions and stir-fry to soften slightly (about a minute). Remove from pan.

5. Add the second quantity of oil and heat. Add celery and water chestnuts. Stir-fry a minute or two. Remove from pan.

6. Add the remaining oil and heat. Then add chicken. Stir-fry until it loses its pinkness and turns white. Return the vegetables. Stir-fry a minute or two more to blend flavors and reheat.

7. Add the pineapple cubes and juice. Stir-fry only to heat pineapple through. Serve at once.

STIR-FRIED CHICKEN AND WALNUTS

1 *chicken (2 pounds)*
1 *tablespoon cornstarch*
2 *tablespoons soy sauce*
3 *tablespoons medium-dry sherry*
½ *teaspoon salt*
⅛ *pound mushrooms*
6 *water chestnuts*
½ *cup celery*

1 *medium onion*
1 *tablespoon oil*
1 *cup blanched walnuts*
2 *tablespoons oil*
½ *teaspoon salt*
2 *tablespoons oil*
1 *tablespoon medium-dry sherry*
¼ *cup chicken stock*

1. Skin the chicken. Remove meat from bones and cut in ½-inch cubes. Place in a bowl.

2. In a cup, combine the cornstarch, soy sauce, sherry and salt. Add to chicken and toss to coat. Let stand 15 minutes, turning chicken occasionally.

3. Meanwhile slice the mushrooms and the water chestnuts. Dice the celery and onion to match the chicken cubes.

4. Heat a wok or skillet. Add the first quantity of oil and heat. Add the walnuts and brown about a minute over medium heat. (Watch for burning.) Remove from pan.

5. Heat the second quantity of oil. Add the remaining salt and vegetables, stir-frying until they begin to soften (about 2 minutes). Remove from pan.

6. Rinse, then reheat pan. Add the last of the oil and heat, then add chicken. Stir-fry until it loses its pinkness and turns white. Sprinkle with remaining sherry. Stir-fry a minute more.

7. Return vegetables to pan. Add the stock and heat. Cover

pan, reduce heat and cook another 2 minutes. Stir in walnuts and serve at once.

STIR-FRIED CHICKEN LIVERS AND ALMONDS

1 *pound chicken livers*	2 *tablespoons medium-dry*
Water to cover	*sherry*
2 *scallions*	½ *teaspoon salt*
2 *slices fresh ginger root*	1 *tablespoon cornstarch*
1 *garlic clove*	⅓ *cup cold chicken stock*
1 *tablespoon brown sugar*	*Flour*
2 *tablespoons soy sauce*	2 *tablespoons oil*

½ *cup blanched almonds*

1. Trim fat and gristle from the chicken livers. Bring the water to a boil. Add livers, parboil 2 minutes, then drain. Cut each in bite-sized pieces.

2. Mince the scallions and ginger root. Put in a bowl. Crush garlic slightly and add. Stir in the brown sugar, soy sauce, sherry and salt. Add chicken livers to bowl, tossing to coat. Let stand about an hour, turning them occasionally.

3. Drain livers, reserving marinade. Combine marinade with the cornstarch and stock. Dredge livers lightly in the flour.

4. Heat a wok or skillet. Add the oil and heat. Stir in the almonds and brown lightly over medium heat. (Watch for burning.) Remove from pan.

5. Turn heat to high. Add a little more oil if necessary, then chicken livers, stir-frying until golden. Remove from pan.

6. Restir marinade-cornstarch mixture and add to pan. Bring quickly to a boil, stirring until thickened. Return livers, stir-frying only to reheat. Garnish with almonds and serve at once.

STIR-FRIED SHRIMP AND MIXED VEGETABLES

1 *pound medium shrimp*	3 *stalks celery*
Salted water	10 *water chestnuts*
2 *slices fresh ginger root*	5 *mushrooms*
2 *tablespoons soy sauce*	1 *tablespoon cornstarch*
1 *tablespoon medium-dry*	¼ *cup cold chicken stock*
sherry	3 *tablespoons oil*
¼ *teaspoon salt*	¼ *teaspoon salt*

1. Let shrimp stand in salted water for 15 minutes, then shell and devein. Place in a bowl.

2. Mince the ginger root and combine in a cup with the soy sauce, sherry and salt. Add to shrimp, tossing gently to coat. Let stand about 15 minutes, turning shrimp occasionally.

3. Meanwhile cut the celery in 1-inch lengths, quarter the water chestnuts, slice the mushrooms. In a cup, blend the cornstarch and stock to a paste.

4. Heat a wok or skillet. Add the oil and heat, then the remaining salt. Add vegetables and stir-fry to soften slightly (about 2 or 3 minutes).

5. Add shrimp. Stir-fry until they turn pinkish (about 2 minutes).

6. Restir cornstarch paste and add to pan. Continue stir-frying until liquids thicken. Serve at once.

STIR-FRIED SHRIMP AND PEAS

½ pound medium shrimp
Salted water to cover
Few drops of ginger juice
1 tablespoon medium-dry sherry
½ egg white
1 tablespoon cornstarch
1 pound fresh green peas

Water to cover
1 tablespoon salt
Oil for deep-frying
2 tablespoons oil
½ teaspoon salt
1 tablespoon medium-dry sherry
Pinch of sugar

1. Let shrimp stand in the salted water for 15 minutes, then shell and devein. Place in a bowl.

2. Combine the ginger juice, sherry, egg white and cornstarch, blending them well. Add to shrimp and toss to coat.

3. Shell the peas. Bring the remaining water to a boil. Add the salt, then peas, and parboil until bright green (about 2 minutes). Drain. Cool in a colander under cold running water and drain again.

4. Meanwhile heat the deep-frying oil. Add shrimp and deep-fry until pinkish-gold. Drain on paper toweling. Pour off oil.

5. Reheat wok or skillet. Add the remaining oil and heat. Add the remaining salt, then shrimp and peas, stir-frying only to reheat. Sprinkle with the remaining sherry and sugar and stir-fry a few times to blend flavors. Serve at once.

STIR-FRIED SCALLOPS AND PEPPERS

1 pound scallops
1 tablespoon cornstarch
2 tablespoons medium-dry sherry
¼ cup chicken stock

2 green peppers
2 scallions
2 tablespoons oil
½ teaspoon salt

1. Slice the scallops and put in a bowl. In a cup, combine the cornstarch and sherry. Add to scallops, tossing gently to coat. Let stand 15 minutes, turning scallops occasionally.

2. Meanwhile cut the peppers in half, discarding seeds and membranes, then dice. Chop the scallions coarsely.

3. Heat a wok or skillet. Add the oil and heat. Add scallions and stir-fry a few times. Add scallops and stir-fry until half cooked (about 2 minutes).

4. Add salt, then green pepper. Stir-fry a few times to soften slightly. Add the stock and heat. Cover pan, reduce heat to medium and cook until peppers soften but are still bright green and crunchy (about 2 minutes). Serve at once.

STIR-FRIED CAULIFLOWER

1 *head cauliflower*	¼ *cup chicken stock*
Water to cover	1 *tablespoon medium-dry*
1 *tablespoon salt*	*sherry*
2 *slices fresh ginger root*	1 *teaspoon soy sauce*
4 *to* 5 *water chestnuts*	1 *teaspoon oyster sauce*
2 *scallions*	2 *tablespoons oil*
2 *tablespoons ham*	2 *teaspoons cornstarch*
1 *tablespoon water*	

1. Break the cauliflower into flowerets. Bring the water to a boil. Add the salt, then flowerets, and parboil 2 or 3 minutes. Drain. Cool in a colander under cold running water. Drain again.

2. Slightly crush the ginger root. Slice the water chestnuts. Separately mince the scallions and ham.

3. In a small bowl, combine the stock, sherry, soy sauce and oyster sauce.

4. Heat a wok or skillet. Add the oil and heat. Add ginger root and brown lightly. Add scallions and water chestnuts, stir-frying a few times. Gradually but quickly add cauliflower, stir-frying to coat with oil and heat.

5. Quickly stir in the stock mixture and bring to a boil.

Cover pan, reduce heat to medium and cook until cauliflower is done but still crunchy (about 3 minutes).

6. Meanwhile blend the cornstarch and water to a paste. Then stir into pan to thicken liquids. Stir-fry only to coat vegetable, then transfer cauliflower to a bowl. Sprinkle with ham and serve at once.

STIR-FRIED SPINACH

1 *pound fresh spinach*	2 *tablespoons oil*
1 *garlic clove*	½ *teaspoon salt*

1. Wash spinach well, discarding tough stems. Drain in a colander to remove excess water. Crush the garlic slightly.
2. Heat a wok or skillet. Add the oil and heat, then add the salt and garlic. Brown garlic slightly. Add spinach by the handful and stir-fry until softened but still bright green. Serve at once.

HAM FRIED RICE

3 *to 4 cups cold cooked rice*	½ *cup blanched almonds*
¼ *pound ham*	1 *tablespoon oil*
2 *medium onions*	3 *tablespoons oil*
3 *eggs*	½ *teaspoon salt*
½ *teaspoon salt*	1 *tablespoon soy sauce*

1. Break up and separate the rice by hand or with a fork. Shred the ham and onions. Beat the eggs with the first quantity of salt.
2. Sliver the almonds. Heat a wok or skillet. Add the first quantity of oil and heat. Add almonds and stir-fry a minute or two over medium heat to brown. (Watch for burning.) Remove from pan and set aside.
3. Reheat pan. Add the remaining oil and heat. Pour in eggs. When half-set, add rice and the remaining salt. Stir-fry rapidly to coat rice with eggs.

4. Add ham, then onion shreds, stir-frying to blend in. Sprinkle with the soy sauce and continue stir-frying until mixture is well blended and heated through.

5. Stir in almonds and serve at once.

CRABMEAT FRIED RICE

2 tomatoes
Boiling water
3 cups cold cooked rice
1 cup cooked crabmeat
4 scallions
4 water chestnuts

2 eggs
¼ teaspoon salt
2 teaspoons medium-dry
  sherry
2 tablespoons chicken stock
1 tablespoon soy sauce

2 tablespoons oil

1. Plunge each tomato into rapidly boiling water for about 20 seconds. Peel at once, then cut in small cubes.

2. Break up and separate the rice by hand or with a fork. Pick over and flake the crabmeat. Cut the scallions in ½-inch sections. Dice the water chestnuts.

3. Beat the eggs lightly with the salt and sherry. In a cup, combine the stock and soy sauce.

4. Heat a wok or skillet. Add the oil and heat. Add rice and stir-fry to coat with oil and heat through thoroughly. Add crabmeat and blend in.

5. Push rice aside, making a well in the center of the pan. Pour in egg mixture and—while it's still liquid—stir-fry rice to coat with egg.

6. Add tomatoes, stir-frying only to heat through. Restir stock mixture and quickly blend in. Serve at once.

YANGCHOW NOODLES

½ *pound lean pork*	½ *pound noodles*
2 *to* 3 *celery stalks*	*Water to cover*
2 *scallions*	1 *tablespoon salt*
6 *mushrooms*	2 *tablespoons oil*
1 *tablespoon cornstarch*	½ *teaspoon salt*
1 *tablespoon water*	1 *tablespoon medium-dry*
1 *teaspoon soy sauce*	*sherry*
½ *cup chicken stock*	

1. Cut the pork in thin slices, then into strips. Cut the celery and scallions in similar strips. Slice the mushrooms. In a cup, combine the cornstarch, water and soy sauce.

2. Bring the water to cover the noodles to a boil. Add the salt, then noodles, and cook until softened but still firm. Drain in a colander; rinse briefly under cold running water. Drain again. Transfer noodles to a double boiler to rewarm.

3. Heat a wok or skillet. Add the oil and heat. Add the remaining salt, then pork strips. Stir-fry until they lose their pinkness and begin to brown. Sprinkle with the sherry and stir-fry a few times more.

4. Add celery and scallions, stir-frying to soften slightly. Add mushrooms, then the stock, and bring to a boil. Cover pan, reduce heat to medium and cook meat and vegetables 2 to 3 minutes. Meanwhile transfer noodles to individual serving bowls.

5. Restir cornstarch mixture and add to pan. Stir-fry over medium-high heat until the liquids thicken. Spoon meat and vegetable mixture over noodles. Serve at once.

STIR-FRIED CHICKEN LIVERS WITH NOODLES

½ pound noodles	*1 tablespoon cornstarch*
Water to cover	*2 tablespoons water*
1 tablespoon salt	*2 teaspoons soy sauce*
1 tablespoon oil	*2 tablespoons oil*
1 pound chicken livers	*2 tablespoons oil*
2 to 3 celery stalks	*½ teaspoon salt*
1 medium onion	*¼ cup chicken stock*

1. Bring the water to a boil. Add the salt, then the noodles. Cook until softened but still firm. Drain in a colander. Rinse under cold running water. Drain again. Add the oil to noodles, tossing to coat. Refrigerate several hours to chill.

2. Trim fat and gristle from the chicken livers, then cut in bite-sized pieces. Chop the celery and onion coarsely. In a cup, combine the cornstarch, remaining water and soy sauce.

3. Heat a wok or skillet. Add the second quantity of oil and heat. Divide chilled noodles into two or three batches and

pan-fry each until brown on both sides, adding more oil if necessary. Transfer to a preheated serving platter and keep warm.

4. Add the last of the oil and heat. Add the remaining salt, then the chicken livers. Stir-fry to brown lightly. Add celery and onion, stir-frying to soften slightly.

5. Add the stock and bring to a boil. Cover pan. Reduce heat and cook covered 2 to 3 minutes.

6. Restir cornstarch paste and add to pan. Stir-fry over medium-high heat until liquids thicken. Spoon chicken liver and vegetable mixture over noodles. Serve at once.

❀ *Deep-frying* ❀

JUST ABOUT EVERYONE deep-fries—the French, Germans, Italians, Americans and Chinese. When they plunge their ingredients into the searing oil, they all face the same challenge: to have the heat reach and cook the inside of the food before the outside—which is in direct contact with the oil—gets so ferociously hot that it burns.

The Chinese, who deep-fry with a difference, meet this challenge in a variety of ways: They cut the food in bite-sized pieces and so shorten the distance the heat must travel from the surface to the center. They marinate their ingredients in soy sauce and wine mixtures. (This tenderizes as well as flavors them so that less time is needed in the oil.) The Chinese double-fry as well, putting the food in the oil in two separate stages and letting it cool in between. (While the outside temperature decreases, the inside holds the heat and goes right on cooking.)

In addition, the Chinese protect their meat, seafood and poultry—as other cooks do—either by dredging them in cornstarch or flour or by enclosing them in batter. The coatings not only shield the vulnerable surfaces against the depredations of the oil but seal in the natural juices of the food as well.

PAPER-WRAPPING

The Chinese have developed yet another—and quite unexpected—way to coat their ingredients. They use small paper envelopes to enclose and insulate the bite-sized morsels. And, unlike other coatings, the wrappings add no calories at all.

A porous paper is used—wax paper, bond, parchment or oriental rice paper—never plastic wrap, which melts, or aluminum foil, which isn't porous. The ingredients are always marinated first, then drained and put in the envelopes, usually with a bit of garnish. The packets are then briefly immersed in the oil to deep-fry.

The envelopes, being simple to assemble, can be made quickly. First, the paper is cut in squares ranging in size from 4 to 8 inches, with the smaller ones used for hors d'oeuvres, the larger ones for bulky ingredients such as jumbo shrimp. Paper-wrapping is done as follows:

1. Place each square of paper on a flat surface with the lower corner pointing toward you. Brush the center lightly with oil—peanut, sesame or other vegetable oil.

2. Place a piece or two of the ingredient well below the center line. (Depending on the size of the food and the size of the paper, one or two bite-sized morsels will fit into each envelope.) Place the garnish over the ingredient.

3. Fold the bottom corner up to cover the ingredient. This should form a triangle whose tip is about an inch from the topmost corner. Crease the paper to hold.

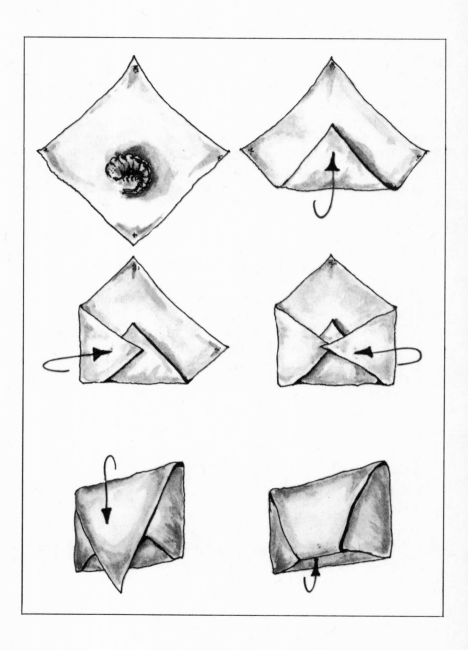

4. Fold the left corner, then the right corner over so they meet in the middle, overlapping slightly, envelope style. Keep the corners square. Crease the sides to hold.

5. At this point, you should have a small envelope with a pointed flap. Fold the envelope in half horizontally so the flap extends beyond the bottom. To secure the packet, tuck the flap underneath the folded corners (which have formed a slot between the bottom edges). Crease to hold.

6. Line up the envelopes side by side. They're now ready for the cooking process.

Depending on the size and density of the ingredient, deep-frying will take from two to five minutes. For even cooking, the packet is turned over once. To check for doneness, a packet is opened and its contents sampled.

Packets must never be left in the oil more than five minutes or they'll burn. If they require longer cooking, they're lifted out after two or three minutes, permitted to cool briefly, then returned to the oil. If wire baskets are used, the envelopes may be deep-fried in several batches, a few minutes each, then the entire lot deep-fried a few minutes more.

As with stir-fried foods, paper-wrapped ingredients are served at once. The packets are well drained and pressed gently with a fork to remove the last few drops of oil. The still unopened envelopes are then heaped on a platter over a bed of lettuce strips or surrounded by fresh vegetables cut in decorative shapes. Each diner picks up one envelope at a time, lifts the paper flap with chopsticks or fork and extracts the tasty morsel. Because the envelope remains closed until the last moment, all the heat, delicacy and flavor of the food are thus retained.

Paper-wrapping is a versatile technique, lending itself to countless variations both as to the contents and their seasonings. The ingredients most frequently prepared this way are white-meat chicken, fish fillets and shrimp. Beef is used less often, and pork rarely.

PAPER-WRAPPED CHICKEN

1 *large or 2 small chicken*
 breasts
2 *tablespoons medium-dry*
 sherry
2 *teaspoons soy sauce*

½ *teaspoon salt*
¼ *teaspoon sugar*
⅛ *teaspoon white pepper*
1 *scallion*
Oil for deep-frying

1. Skin and bone the chicken breast, then cut in bite-sized rectangles.

2. In a bowl, combine the sherry, soy sauce, salt, sugar and pepper. Add chicken pieces and let stand about 30 minutes, turning them occasionally. Meanwhile cut the scallion stalk in thin diagonal slices.

3. Drain chicken and enclose one or two pieces in each paper packet, along with a slice of scallion. Meanwhile heat the oil.

4. Deep-fry packets until chicken is done. Drain and serve at once.

NOTE: A wide variety of garnishes in addition to the scallion slices can be used, such as shredded snow peas, sprigs of parsley, pine nuts or slivers of ginger root, celery or ham.

PAPER-WRAPPED FISH

½ *pound fish fillets*
2 *tablespoons medium-dry*
 sherry
½ *teaspoon salt*

Dash of white pepper
½ *teaspoon ginger juice*
1 *scallion*
Oil for deep-frying

1. Cut the fish fillets diagonally in thin slices, then into bite-sized strips.

2. In a bowl, combine the sherry, salt, pepper and ginger juice. Add fish strips and let stand about 30 minutes, turning them occasionally. Meanwhile cut the scallion stalk in thin, diagonal slices.

3. Drain fish and enclose a strip or two in a paper packet, along with a scallion slice. Meanwhile heat the oil.

4. Deep-fry packets only until fish is cooked through. Drain and serve at once.

NOTE: White-meat fish, such as bass, sole or flounder, is preferable here.

PAPER-WRAPPED SHRIMP

4 jumbo shrimp
¼ sweet red pepper
1 scallion
1 slice fresh ginger root
1 garlic clove

2 tablespoons medium-dry
   sherry
½ teaspoon salt
⅛ teaspoon white pepper
Oil for deep-frying

1. Shell and devein the shrimp. Cut the red pepper in small strips. Sliver the scallion; shred the ginger root; mince the garlic.

2. Combine garlic in a bowl with the sherry, salt and pepper. Add shrimp and let stand 30 minutes, turning them occasionally.

3. Drain shrimp and enclose each in a paper packet along with some red pepper, scallion and ginger root. Meanwhile heat the oil.

4. Deep-fry packets until the shrimp turn pinkish. Drain and serve at once.

PAPER-WRAPPED BEEF

½ *pound flank steak*	1 *tablespoon sherry*
1 *scallion*	½ *teaspoon salt*
2 *to 3 snow peas*	*Pinch of sugar*
2 *tablespoons soy sauce*	*Few drops of sesame oil*

Oil for deep-frying

1. Cut the beef against the grain in thin slices, then into bite-sized rectangles. Slice the scallion thinly on the diagonal. Shred the snow peas.

2. In a bowl, combine the soy sauce, sherry, salt, sugar and sesame oil. Add beef and let stand about 30 minutes, turning it occasionally.

3. Drain beef and enclose in individual paper packets along with some shredded snow peas and a slice of scallion. Meanwhile heat the oil.

4. Deep-fry packets until beef is cooked to desired doneness. Drain and serve at once.

COATING THE INGREDIENTS

When the Chinese insulate their meat, poultry and seafood more conventionally by dredging them in cornstarch or enclosing them in batter, they cut the ingredients in bite-sized pieces or on occasion, as with fish, leave them whole. Sometimes the meat and seafood are minced and shaped into small meatballs or fish balls.

Conventionally coated or not, before any of these go into the pan, they must always be at room temperature so as not to lower the temperature of the oil too abruptly. For the same reason they are gradually added—a piece or two at a time, rather than all at once. As for the batter, moderation is recommended. Too much batter absorbs too much oil; too little doesn't protect the food properly. In either case, the results are distressingly greasy and soggy. When food is properly deep-fried, it becomes dry, crisp and golden on the outside, tender and still moist on the inside.

Equally important is the temperature of the oil. If it's not hot enough, the surface crust will take too long to form. If it's too hot, the crust will form too quickly and char before the inside is cooked through.

Deep-frying oil is heated slowly. As a rule, its temperatures are best between 350° and 375°F. At the lower range the oil is ready for fish, kidneys and the white meat of chicken. At the higher range, for beef or pork. If the food is precooked in any way, higher temperatures are indicated. If the food is raw, lower temperatures are used. (Some cooks turn up the heat at the very end of the process for a final crisping.)

The temperatures can be checked with or without a thermometer. If a piece of potato dropped into the oil sinks to the bottom, the oil is too cool. If it rises but doesn't bounce about, the oil is at the lower end of the temperature range. If it bounces and begins to brown, the temperature is about right. If it browns almost at once, the oil is too hot.

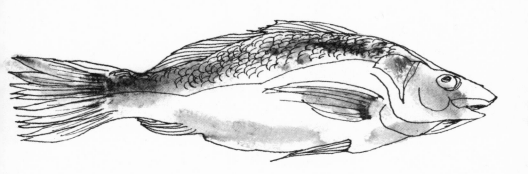

Peanut oil is a frequent deep-frying medium, although soy and other vegetable oils are used as well. (Never olive oil; its flavor is too distinctive.)

Peanut oil has a number of distinct advantages: It can cook at high temperatures without burning. It doesn't absorb food odors and can be reused several times. It keeps indefinitely without refrigeration. (When cooled, it should be strained through a double thickness of cheesecloth, transferred to a container and kept covered.)

Generally, six to eight cups of oil are used for deep-frying. This is sufficient for whole fish and poultry and enables cut-up ingredients to float to the top when done. Smaller quantities may be used as well, depending on the nature of the food and the size of the pan. Two inches of oil, for example, are sufficient for meatballs and fish balls. Or one might get by with 1½ inches by ladling the hot oil over the ingredients, then turning them over and repeating the process.

The most economical pan for deep-frying is the Chinese wok: Its small base and sloping sides make it possible to expose the oil's largest cooking surface. In the absence of a wok, a pan at least five inches deep may be used. (This allows for two inches of oil and three inches of head room to keep the oil from boiling over.) The pan's diameter should be large enough to keep the batter-coated ingredients from crowding together and clumping. If its diameter is small, the food must be cooked in smaller batches.

As for suitable utensils, long-handled forks, slotted spoons and bamboo chopsticks are all useful for turning the ingredients over and lifting them out of the oil. These can also be used to remove free-floating bits of batter and scraps of food that would otherwise burn and smoke disagreeably. Bamboo chopsticks are particularly helpful for shaking off excess batter and for separating the batter-coated ingredients from each other as they cook.

Suitable for draining the food are wire baskets, colanders, strainers or sieves. The Chinese often use round mesh strainers made of brass with long bamboo handles, which come in a wide range of sizes. Their shallowness makes it easy to transfer whole fish and poultry into the oil and out again.

Chinese double-frying, used with both batter-coated and paper-wrapped foods, has a number of advantages. Not only does it slow down the cooking of the surface, it also makes the deep-fried food particularly crisp. Double-frying is done in three stages: (1) deep-frying, (2) cooling and (3) refrying.

In stage 1 the food is cooked almost to the point of doneness but removed from the oil while still pale golden. In stage

2 it's cooled for a minimum of 5 or 10 minutes to a maximum of about 10 hours. (During the longer intervals, it's refrigerated. Then, about an hour before the completion of cooking, it's gradually returned to room temperature.) In stage 3 the oil is reheated to a slightly higher temperature (since the food is already cooked) and the ingredients returned briefly to the pan for a second frying. When golden brown and very crisp, they are removed and drained.

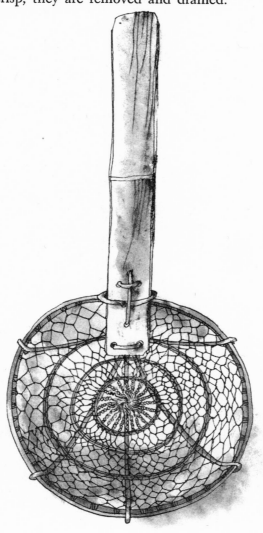

Chinese restaurants generally double-fry their egg rolls, pork and whole fish. (This is how they're able to serve them so quickly.) Home cooks who wish to get as much preparation as possible done in advance may do the same.

Deep-frying must be approached with care and caution. Should any moisture come in contact with the hot oil, spattering will inevitably result. It's therefore advisable to have a pot lid or colander nearby to use as a cover until the spattering stops. If there's a considerable amount of frying to do, one should cover the hands and arms with a thin coating of oil. (Dry skin burns more easily.) Or else one can protect the hands with sturdy rubber gloves.

THE SWEET-AND-SOUR SAUCE

The Chinese seldom serve their deep-fried meats and seafood plain. They embellish them with sweet-and-sour sauces or accompany them with aromatic salt-and-pepper dips.

Unlike other Chinese sauces, which are an integral part of

the dish, sweet-and-sour sauces are always prepared separately and added at the end. With their curious juxtaposition of pungent and subtle flavorings, they appeal both to those who know a great deal about Chinese cooking and those who don't.

Sweet-and-sour sauces call for sugar, vinegar, soy sauce, fruit juices, tomato sauce and seasonings to be blended, brought to a boil and then thickened with cornstarch paste. (A heavy enamel or iron pot is best since aluminum and vinegar tend to be incompatible.) The sweet-and-sour mixtures of Canton feature fruits and vegetables, such as pineapple, tomato, onion, carrot and green pepper—cut in chunks or slivers. The sauces of Shanghai do not.

When properly prepared, a sweet-and-sour sauce is glistening, translucent and syrupy. Its taste is mildly sharp and quite refreshing. Sweetness and tartness can be adjusted by modifying the sugar-vinegar ratio. The sauce may be made more pungent with a bit of minced orange peel or made darker with a tablespoon or two of heavy soy sauce or hotter with some chili peppers, as the Szechwanese prefer it.

Since both the food and the sweet-and-sour sauce must be bracingly hot when served, their preparation should be synchronized so both are ready at the same time. The best way to do this is to assemble—but not cook—all the sauce ingredients before deep-frying actually begins. Then, while the food crisps in the oil, the sauce is heated through and thickened. (This is one sauce that is always thickened.)

If necessary, deep-fried foods can be kept warm briefly in a 180° to 200°F. oven. Or if the ingredients are small both in size and in quantity, they can be added to the sweet-and-sour sauce itself and reheated in the pan a minute or two. If reheated any longer, they lose their coveted crispness.

An equally interesting but less well-known accompaniment for deep-fried foods is the piquant salt-and-pepper dip. This aromatic mixture, which can be served either with batter-coated or paper-wrapped foods, is set out a tablespoon or two at a time, in a separate dip dish or on the side of the serving platter itself.

SWEET-AND-SOUR PORK

1 *pound lean pork*	*Sweet-and-sour sauce*
2 *tablespoons medium-dry*	¼ *cup flour*
sherry	¼ *cup cornstarch*
1 *tablespoon soy sauce*	*Pinch of salt*
¼ *teaspoon salt*	4 *tablespoons water*
¼ *teaspoon sugar*	1 *large egg*
⅛ *teaspoon pepper*	*Oil for deep-frying*

1. Trim the pork of its excess fat and cut in 1-inch cubes. Put meat in a bowl and sprinkle with the sherry, soy sauce, salt, sugar and pepper. Toss pork and let stand about 30 minutes, turning it occasionally.

2. Meanwhile prepare and assemble the sweet-and-sour ingredients as indicated in steps 1 and 2 of the recipe below.

3. Next, combine the flour, cornstarch, salt and water to make a batter. Beat the egg and blend in. Meanwhile heat the oil.

4. Drain pork, then dip in the batter to coat on all sides. Add meat gradually to oil and deep-fry until crisp, golden and completely cooked through (about 5 minutes).

5. Meanwhile complete the sweet-and-sour sauce as in steps 3 and 4 below.

6. Drain pork on paper toweling and transfer to a serving dish. Pour over the sweet-and-sour sauce and serve.

SWEET-AND-SOUR SAUCE

2 *green peppers*	3 *tablespoons sugar*
1 *large onion*	2 *tablespoons tomato sauce*
3 *slices canned pineapple*	½ *cup vinegar*
1 *garlic clove*	1 *cup pineapple juice*
1 *tablespoon cornstarch*	½ *teaspoon salt*
3 *tablespoons water*	2 *tablespoons oil*

1. Cut the peppers in half, discarding their seeds and membranes, then cut in 1-inch squares. Cut the onion and pine-

apple in similar cubes. Mince the garlic. In a cup, blend the cornstarch and water to a paste.

2. In an enamel saucepan, blend the sugar, tomato sauce, vinegar, pineapple juice and salt.

3. Bring the saucepan ingredients slowly to a boil, stirring occasionally. Meanwhile heat a wok or skillet. Add the oil and heat. Add garlic, then onion, then green pepper, stir-frying continuously to heat through and soften slightly (about 2½ minutes). Add pineapple cubes only to heat.

4. Add the stir-fried ingredients to the heated sauce. Re-stir the cornstarch paste and quickly stir in over medium-high heat to thicken. Pour sauce over crisp deep-fried pork as indicated.

DEEP-FRIED PORK BALLS

1½ pounds pork	Dash of pepper
6 water chestnuts	1 egg
1 scallion	1 egg
½ teaspoon salt	Cornstarch
Oil for deep-frying	

1. Mince or grind the pork with some of its fat. Put in a bowl. Mince the water chestnuts and scallion stalk and add, along with the salt and pepper.

2. Separate the first egg. Beat its yolk and add to meat.

Blend the mixture but do not overwork. Shape into walnut-sized meatballs.

3. Beat the egg white with the second egg. Dip meatballs first into egg, then in the cornstarch to coat. Repeat process a second time. Meanwhile heat the oil.

4. Add meatballs to oil gradually and carefully so they don't clump together. Deep-fry until golden brown and cooked through (about 8 minutes). Cut into a meatball to check for doneness. (If it's still pink, cook a while longer.) Drain on paper toweling. Serve hot with mustard or a salt-and-pepper dip.

NOTE: Deep-fried pork balls can also be served with a sweet-and-sour sauce poured over.

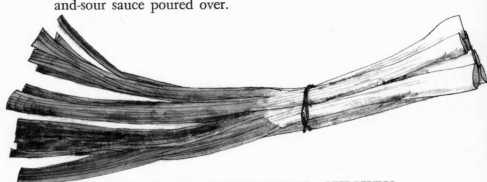

DEEP-FRIED EIGHT-PIECE CHICKEN

1 chicken (2 pounds)	1 tablespoon soy sauce
1 scallion stalk	½ teaspoon salt
1 garlic clove	½ teaspoon sugar
2 slices fresh ginger root	Oil for deep-frying
2 tablespoons sherry	Cornstarch

1. Cut the chicken in half lengthwise with a cleaver or poultry shears, then cut each half in four roughly equal pieces. Place them in a bowl.

2. Cut the scallion in ¼-inch sections. Crush the garlic and the ginger root slightly. Add to chicken.

3. In a cup, blend together the sherry, soy sauce, salt and sugar. Pour the mixture over chicken and toss to coat. Let

stand about 30 minutes, turning chicken occasionally. Drain, discarding marinade. Meanwhile heat the oil.

4. Dredge chicken pieces lightly in the cornstarch, then add to oil. Deep-fry until all are pale golden (about 5 minutes). Remove and let cool.

5. Reheat oil. Return chicken and deep-fry until crisp and golden brown (about another 2 minutes). Drain on paper toweling. Serve hot with a salt-and-pepper dip.

DEEP-FRIED CHICKEN SQUARES

1 *chicken (2 pounds)*	2 *tablespoons soy sauce*
1 *medium onion*	1 *teaspoon salt*
3 *tablespoons medium-dry*	½ *teaspoon sugar*
sherry	*Oil for deep-frying*
Flour	

1. Cut the chicken in half lengthwise with a cleaver or poultry shears, then cut—bones and all—in 2-inch squares. Place in a bowl.

2. Coarsely chop the onion and blend with the sherry, soy sauce, salt and sugar.

3. Pour the mixture over chicken pieces, tossing gently to coat. Let stand an hour, turning chicken occasionally.

4. Heat the oil. Drain chicken, then dip each piece in the flour to coat. Deep-fry until golden brown (about 3 minutes). Drain on paper toweling and serve.

DEEP-FRIED WALNUT CHICKEN

1 *large or 2 small chicken*	½ *teaspoon salt*
breasts	*Dash of white pepper*
1 *cup blanched walnuts*	*Oil for deep-frying*
2 *tablespoons medium-dry*	2 *egg whites*
sherry	4 *tablespoons cornstarch*

1. Skin and bone the chicken breasts, then cut in rectangles 1½ by 2½ inches. Coarsely chop the walnuts.

2. Put chicken pieces in a bowl. Sprinkle with the sherry, salt and pepper. Let stand about 15 minutes, turning them occasionally. Meanwhile heat the oil.

3. Lightly beat the egg whites, then blend in the cornstarch to make a batter, thinning with water if necessary. Dip chicken pieces in batter to coat, then in chopped walnuts.

4. Gradually add to oil and deep-fry until golden brown (about 1½ minutes). Drain on paper toweling. Serve with a salt-and-pepper dip.

DEEP-FRIED CHICKEN LIVERS

1 *pound chicken livers*	½ *cup flour*
2 *tablespoons soy sauce*	*Pinch of baking powder*
1 *tablespoon sherry*	*Oil for deep-frying*

1. Trim fat and gristle from the chicken livers, then divide each in three parts.

2. Combine the soy sauce and sherry and add to chicken livers, tossing to coat. Let stand 15 minutes, turning occasionally.

3. Blend the flour and baking powder and thin with water to make a smooth batter. Meanwhile heat the oil.

4. Dip chicken livers in batter to coat, then deep-fry until cooked through and golden. Serve with a salt-and-pepper dip.

DEEP-FRIED SWEET-AND-SOUR FISH

1 *whole fish* (1½ *to 2 pounds*)	*Sweet-and-sour sauce*
	½ *cup cornstarch*
2 *tablespoons soy sauce*	1 *egg*
1 *tablespoon sherry*	*Oil for deep-frying*

1. Have the fish cleaned and scaled, with head and tail left intact. Rinse in cold water; dry with paper toweling. Score fish on each side with several diagonal slashes about ¼ inch deep. (These will speed up both marinating and cooking.)

2. Combine the soy sauce and sherry and brush over fish. Let stand about 30 minutes.

3. Meanwhile prepare and assemble the ingredients for the sweet-and-sour sauce as indicated in steps 1 and 2 of the recipe below.

4. Drain fish and pat dry with paper toweling. Spread the cornstarch on a sheet of waxed paper. Lightly beat the egg and brush over fish; then roll fish in cornstarch to coat. Shake off any excess. Meanwhile heat the oil.

5. Hold fish by the tail with one hand and support its body with the other. Gently lower into oil head first. As the underside cooks, carefully ladle hot oil over the top.

6. Deep-fry 5 to 7 minutes on each side, or until the fish is cooked through and golden brown. Meanwhile complete the sweet-and-sour sauce as in steps 3, 4 and 5 below.

7. Drain fish on paper toweling. Transfer to a preheated serving platter. Pour the sweet-and-sour sauce over and serve.

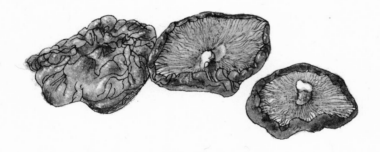

SWEET-AND-SOUR SAUCE

3 dried black mushrooms	*3 tablespoons tomato sauce*
2 scallions	*1 tablespoon soy sauce*
1 small bamboo shoot	*½ teaspoon salt*
1 small carrot	*¾ cup chicken stock*
2 slices fresh ginger root	*1 tablespoon cornstarch*
6 tablespoons sugar	*2 tablespoons water*
4 tablespoons vinegar	*2 tablespoons oil*

1. Soak the mushrooms in hot water to soften (about 30 minutes), then shred. Shred the scallion stalks and mince their green tops. Also shred the bamboo shoot, carrot and ginger root.

2. In an enamel saucepan, blend the sugar, vinegar, tomato sauce, soy sauce, salt and stock. In a cup, blend the cornstarch and water to a paste.

3. Bring the saucepan ingredients to a boil over medium heat, stirring occasionally.

4. Meanwhile heat a wok or skillet. Add the oil and heat,

then add the shredded vegetables. Stir-fry to soften slightly (about 1 or 2 minutes). Add the heated sauce mixture, stirring to blend.

5. Restir the cornstarch paste and quickly stir in to thicken. Pour sauce over the deep-fried fish as indicated. Garnish with green scallion tops and serve.

DEEP-FRIED SHRIMP WITH SHERRY SAUCE

1 *pound raw medium shrimp*	½ *cup cold chicken stock*
1 *large onion*	1 *egg*
1 *tablespoon cornstarch*	3 *tablespoons flour*
1 *tablespoon medium-dry sherry*	½ *teaspoon salt*
	Oil for deep-frying
1 *teaspoon soy sauce*	2 *tablespoons oil*

1. Shell and devein the shrimp. Coarsely chop the onion. In a cup, combine the cornstarch, sherry, soy sauce and stock.

2. Beat the egg. Blend with the flour and salt to make a batter. (Thin with water if necessary.) Meanwhile heat the deep-frying oil.

3. Dip shrimp in the batter to coat, then add gradually and carefully to oil to prevent clumping. Deep-fry until golden brown.

4. Meanwhile, in another pan, add the remaining oil and heat. Add chopped onion and stir-fry to brown. Restir the cornstarch mixture and add, stirring over medium-high heat, until the sauce thickens.

5. Drain shrimp on paper toweling. Transfer to a serving platter. Pour the sauce over and serve.

DEEP-FRIED BUTTERFLY SHRIMP

1 *pound raw jumbo shrimp*	2 *teaspoons medium-dry sherry*
4 *tablespoons flour*	
1 *tablespoon cornstarch*	1 *egg*
½ *teaspoon salt*	2 *slices fresh ginger root*
Oil for deep-frying	

1. Shell the shrimp, leaving their tail segments intact. With the point of a knife, make a slit along the back of each—deep enough to expose the black vein but not so deep as to cut the shrimp in two. (The slit should stop at the tail segment.)

2. Rinse shrimp under cold running water to devein, then pat dry with paper toweling. Press each shrimp gently between the palms of the hands so it spreads open like a butterfly.

3. In a bowl, combine the flour, cornstarch, salt and sherry. Lightly beat the egg and add. Mince the ginger root and add. Beat mixture until it's a smooth batter, thinning with water if necessary. Meanwhile heat the oil.

4. Hold each shrimp by the tail and dip in batter to coat, taking care not to get any on the tail segment. Lower shrimp into oil one at a time; brown lightly on one side, then the other.

5. When shrimp are golden and their tail segments bright red, drain on paper toweling. Transfer shrimp to a round preheated platter and arrange in a circle with their tails pointing outward. Place a dip dish in the center with either a salt-and-pepper mixture or equal parts of soy sauce and tomato sauce heated briefly together.

DEEP-FRIED SHRIMP BALLS

1 *pound raw shrimp*	½ *teaspoon salt*
10 *water chestnuts*	*Oil for deep-frying*
1 *scallion*	1 *egg white*
2 *slices fresh ginger root*	1 *teaspoon cornstarch*
1 *teaspoon medium-dry*	*Lemon wedges*
sherry	*Parsley*

1. Shell, devein and mince the shrimp. Place in a bowl. Mince and add the water chestnuts, scallion and ginger root.

2. Season mixture with the sherry and salt, blending well. Meanwhile heat the oil.

3. Beat the egg white until stiff, then fold in. Sprinkle shrimp mixture with the cornstarch and form into walnut-sized balls.

4. Add shrimp balls gradually to the oil and deep-fry until pinkish gold. Drain on paper toweling.

5. Spear with brightly colored toothpicks. Garnish with the parsley. Serve with the lemon wedges.

NOTE: Deep-fried shrimp balls, like deep-fried pork balls can also be served with a sweet-and-sour sauce.

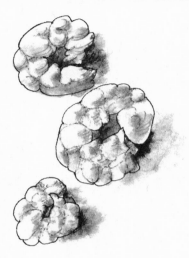

SHRIMP TOAST

½ pound raw shrimp	*1 teaspoon cornstarch*
1 small onion	*½ teaspoon salt*
1 slice fresh ginger root	*Dash of white pepper*
1 egg	*Oil for deep-frying*
1 tablespoon medium-dry	*4 slices white bread*
sherry	*1 tablespoon ham*

1. Shell, devein and mince the shrimp. Place in a bowl. Mince and add the onion and ginger root.

2. Separate the egg, adding the white to shrimp, along with the sherry, cornstarch, salt and pepper. Blend the mixture with a fork or by hand. Meanwhile heat the oil.

3. Trim off the bread crusts, then cut each slice in four equal triangles or rectangles.

4. Spread the shrimp mixture on the bread, working from the edges toward the center. To keep the mixture from sticking, dip the knife or spatula in cold water at intervals. Beat the egg yolk lightly and brush over the top as a glaze.

5. Lower each piece of bread, shrimp-side down, into the oil. Deep-fry until the coating is pinkish and firm (about 2 minutes). Turn over and cook until bread is golden brown (about 1 minute more).

6. Drain on paper toweling. Mince the ham and sprinkle over. Serve at once.

NOTE: Day-old bread is best. Fresh bread is too absorbent.

DEEP-FRIED OYSTERS

2 dozen large oysters	1 teaspoon salt
Boiling water to cover	⅛ teaspoon pepper
2 cups flour	2 tablespoons oil
⅓ cup cornstarch	Oil for deep-frying
2 teaspoons baking powder	Lettuce
1 or 2 tomatoes	

1. Shell the oysters and place in a sieve. Plunge into the boiling water, then lift out immediately. Rinse at once under cold running water.

2. In a bowl, blend together the flour, cornstarch, baking powder, salt and pepper. Stir in the oil. Thin with water to make a smooth batter. Meanwhile heat the remaining oil.

3. Dip each oyster in the batter to coat, then deep-fry until golden brown. Meanwhile shred the lettuce and line a serving platter with the strips. Cut the tomato in wedges.

4. Drain oysters on paper toweling. Arrange on lettuce and garnish with tomatoes. Serve at once, along with a salt-and-pepper dip.

SALT-AND-PEPPER DIP

2 to 3 tablespoons salt   *2 tablespoons peppercorns*

1. Heat a dry, heavy skillet until very hot. Add the salt and whole black peppercorns.

2. Stir constantly over medium heat until salt is slightly brown and pepper is aromatic.

3. Crush in a mortar, breaking up peppercorns, then strain through a fine sieve.

4. Store in a tightly covered container.

NOTE: The salt may be either fine or coarse. Ground black pepper can substitute for the peppercorns.

❀ *Roasting* ❀

THE TRUTH OF the matter is, the Chinese don't roast very much. The method—which originally called for great roaring fires—was out of the question for most people. So the task was taken over by food shops and restaurants, which were able to use their fuel more economically because they cooked in large quantities.

The tradition still continues. One can find in Chinese grocery stores a variety of meats and poultry already roasted. One can see hanging on hooks whole ducks, suckling pigs, pork strips and spareribs. This specialized approach may have narrowed the roasting repertory, but that repertory does include Peking Duck—the pinnacle of Chinese cooking.

Peking Duck with its golden crackling skin is a banquet dish. Its arrival announces the high point of the meal. Only the crisp, choice skin is offered however. (The meat appears either as a separate course or else at another meal altogether.) The rich delicate skin, cut in small rectangles, is presented decoratively on a platter. Accompanying it are Peking doilies, folded neatly in quarters. (They're somewhere between a pancake and a crepe.) Other accompaniments are onion brushes and a spicy hoisin dip.

Each guest picks up a Peking doily, unfolds it, adds a bit of crisp skin, applies some hoisin dip with an onion brush, places the onion brush over the skin, then folds the doily up and over to enclose them both. The diner consumes the delicacy slowly, savoring each bite.

Peking Duck brings to its highest level the Chinese fondness for combining taste, color and texture. It contrasts the rich golden crispness of the skin, the pale soft blandness of the doily, the spicy red sweetness of the hoisin and the crunchy bite of the scallion stalk.

The uniqueness of the dish lies in the fact that the bird is inflated before cooking, making the skin quite taut. This is done by blowing air through a tube inserted into an incision in the neck, thus creating a space between skin and meat. (The bird's head and neck must be intact for this dish. Twine tied tightly around the neck keeps the air from escaping.) The duck is then blanched, glazed with honey or malt sugar and hung to dry for hours in a cool, airy place. When roasted, its skin becomes delicately thin and crisp.

Peking Duck is not a dish for the home cook. Although the plump duck of northern China was a progenitor of Long Island duckling, the recipe itself is not so readily transferable. The duck must be specially reared and force-fed. Long years of apprenticeship are required for its proper preparation. Even slicing the skin is not as simple as it may seem.

Some years ago, when Nikita Khrushchev, then premier of Russia, visited the People's Republic of China, he became so enamored of Peking Duck that he invited some Chinese chefs to Moscow to show their Russian counterparts how to pre-

pare the dish. On their arrival the Chinese found the recipe
couldn't be duplicated. The Russians, it seemed, didn't force-
feed their ducks.

Peking Duck originated in Mongolia but was not perfected
until it reached the city for which it was named sometime
during the Ming dynasty. Peking, China's northern capital,
was the site of the imperial palace. Its enormous wealth at-
tracted the country's greatest chefs, who vied with each other
to create new dishes and produce meals of unrivaled splendor.
Some of these meals, made up of hundreds of courses, took
three days to consume.

In the seventeenth century, when the Ming dynasty was
overthrown, the imperial court was forced to disperse. The
government officials fled south, taking their favorite chefs

with them. Some headed southeast and eventually reached Kwangtung. Others made their way to Szechwan province in the southwest. In their travels the imperial chefs, trained in the classic culinary style of the north, assimilated several other cooking styles as well.

In Szechwan, for example, the northerners were introduced to the hot, peppery foods of the region. They nevertheless retained many light, delicate dishes for their formal banquets. Peking Duck did not make the transition, however. Perhaps the humid Szechwanese climate didn't encourage roasting. At any rate, a variant evolved: mouth-tingling Szechwan Duck, steamed to a tenderness and deep-fried until crunchy and golden.

Those chefs who relocated in Canton, Kwangtung's capital city, were welcomed by a large leisure class, which was placing greater and greater emphasis on fine living and dining as that port city prospered.

The Cantonese were fond of roast duck, too, but rather than inflate it, they filled it with an aromatically seasoned chicken broth. Then they glazed the skin in the manner of Peking and roasted the bird. When done, the rich, burnished duck was chopped into bite-sized sections with some of its seasoned liquid filling spooned over.

The influence of the migrating chefs from the north was but one factor among many in the evolution of Chinese cooking. More influential still was China's great geographical diversity.

China's land mass extends north to topmost Manchuria, south to the jungle border of Vietnam, east to the China Sea and west to the mountains deep in central Asia. Inside this area, equal in size to all of Europe, can be found a tremendous variety of terrains, climates and natural resources. The Yangtze, one of China's longest rivers, roughly divides the country north and south. Northern China is made up of plains and plateaus that know long bitter winters and short hot summers. Southern China, with its hills, mountains and topographical basins, has a mild climate along the coast and

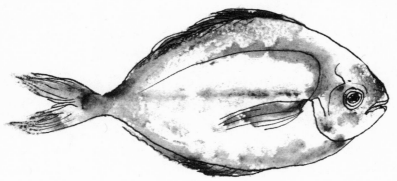

a humid and semitropical one in the interior. The staple northern crop is wheat; the southern, rice.

In addition to their dissimilar natural resources, lack of communication between north and south and problems of preserving food increased the culinary diversity. As many varieties were to develop as there were geographical regions. With the improvement of communications and food preservation, however, the best recipes began to move beyond their local boundaries. Some have since been so adapted, varied and modified that it's no longer possible to indicate their true place of origin.

Despite this continuing assimilation, distinctive regional styles do remain and have been classified in various ways. The simplest classification of all uses the compass-point divisions of north, south, east and west. All involve large areas and, with the exception of Szechwan, are identified with a major city within their boundaries.

The north-northeastern or Peking school includes the former imperial city situated near the Great Wall of China, the provinces of Hopeh, Shantung, Shansi, Shensi and Honan, as well as the vastness of Manchuria and Mongolia. The south-southeastern school, identified as Cantonese cooking, includes Kwangsi and Kwangtung provinces. The eastern or Shanghai school encompasses the cities of Shanghai, Ningpo and Foochow on the east coast and the interior city of Nanking. Also included here are the provinces of Kiangsu, Anhwei, Chekiang,

Kiangsi and Fukien. The west-west central or Szechwanese
school is comprised of Kweichow, Yunnan and Hunan provinces, in addition to Szechwan itself, whose principal city is
Chungking.

The most sophisticated and elegant of all is the northern
or Peking school, which represents classic Chinese cooking.
Its delicate and subtle seasonings emphasize mildness and
lightness rather than richness. Steaming and poaching preserve the food's natural characteristics. Aromatic scallions,
leeks and garlic are frequently used. Wheat flour products
such as noodles, steamed breads and buns are served with
meals. Rice is reserved for banquets.

Characteristic northern dishes include chicken velvet, a
minced chicken breast and egg white combination, and cold
jellied pork. Carp from the Yellow River is favored and often
prepared with a sweet-and-sour sauce. Meats are cooked in
wine stocks. Savory dishes include chicken with chestnuts and
Lion's Head. (The latter, made with large meatballs and leafy
green vegetables, is said to represent the head and mane of
the beast.) Steamed crabs, eaten with fresh ginger root and
vinegar dips are also popular, as are spring rolls, the soft thin
forerunners of egg rolls, and Mu Shu Ro, the shredded pork,
egg and lily bud mixture—stir-fried and served with Peking
doilies.

Roasting, which the brisk northern climate favored, produced not only Peking Duck but the lesser-known Mongolian Barbecue. This dish originated with the nomadic tribes

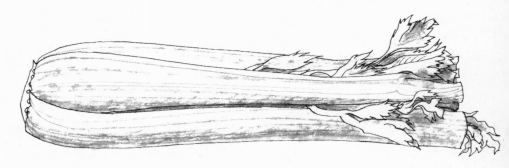

who overran northern China in the thirteenth century and helped introduce the Chinese to lamb. The Mongols cooked their meat over charcoal fires on crude portable grills that they improvised by piercing holes in their metal helmets. Such grills today are still based on the shape of those helmets.

The Mongolian Barbecue calls for the lamb to be cut in thin strips, marinated in a mixture of soy sauce, wine and sesame oil, cooked briefly on each side, then flipped over with long chopsticks. The lamb is eaten on steamed buns along with large helpings of scallions, garlic and shredded vegetables.

Perhaps the most varied Chinese cooking of all is that of the southeastern or Cantonese school. This region's abundant natural resources, rich agricultural land and mild climate all contributed to the versatility.

Cantonese cooks observe the Taoist principle that ingredients should be served as nearly as possible in their natural state. Characteristically, they stir-fry and steam their foods to enhance and blend the natural flavors. Not too many seasonings are used: a light-colored soy sauce that doesn't detract from the fresh brightness of the food, a few herbs and spices, fresh ginger root and wine. A rich, concentrated chicken broth often serves as the cooking medium, while a plentiful sugar supply encourages sweetness in many dishes.

Numerous rivers in Canton and a long coastline provide a great variety of seafood: fish, shrimp, oysters, crabs, lobsters and snails. Specialties include Shark's Fin and Bird's Nest soups, steamed pork and chicken dishes and sweet-and-sour pork. The Cantonese are famous for their "dim sum" or snack tidbits—dumplings and buns filled with meat, poultry, seafood and sweetened bean mixtures. These snacks are eaten any time of the day or night. Besides Cantonese duck, other roasted specialties include barbecued spareribs, pork strips and whole roast pig.

Canton, strategically located at the mouth of the Pearl River facing the South China Sea, was the first Chinese port opened to the outside world when active contact between East and West began in the sixteenth century. The Canton-

ese assimilated many Western influences: They learned to prepare pastries in the French manner, to cook with corn, tomatoes and peanuts. They were the first to migrate to Europe and America and to establish Chinese restaurants there. As a result, Westerners have become more familiar with Cantonese cooking than with any other regional style.

Shanghai, located on the Yangtze River, and facing the East China Sea, was also geographically accessible. Its role as a treaty port made it receptive both to foreign influences and to those of its more immediate neighbors. The cosmopolitan Shanghai or eastern school that evolved was thus a mixture of culinary styles. Along with excellent local dishes, the foods of all nations were served. Meanwhile nearby areas made their own contributions: soy sauce from Fukien, vinegar and ham from Chekiang, wine from Shaoshing, noodles and pastries from Yangchow.

Shanghai cooking, which is rich and elaborately prepared, specializes in braised, gravy-laden dishes, somewhat on the salty side because of their generous use of soy sauce. Meats are often cooked with pickled or salted greens. Rice, the staple here, blandly sets these off.

Shad, perch and mullet are found in the nearby sea. Fresh-water fish and shellfish abound. Many are cooked fresh; some preserved in salt. Specialties of the region include eel in gravy, pig's knuckles and Bird's Nest soup. The people of Shanghai tend to stir-fry their foods somewhat longer than their southern neighbors. And they excel in long-cooked casserole dishes.

Fukien province, south of Shanghai, is sometimes classified separately. Despite being coastal, Fukien was insular and relatively isolated from its nearest neighbors. Its proximity to the sea made oysters, clams and saltwater fish natural favorites. A cuisine based on seafood prevailed. Fukien also has an extensive repertory of clear, light, savory soups, which appear in profusion; two or more are served at family meals, while at banquets as many as three dishes out of 12 might be soup.

Fukien's soy sauce—some say it's China's best—is amply added to dishes that are braised or stewed. Other flavorings include wine, which is subtly used, and a sweet-tasting red condiment made from fermented rice paste. Fukien is also noted for its stir-fried dishes, its roast suckling pig and spring rolls.

NOTE: Sometimes the diverse northern styles of Peking, Shanghai and Tientsin, as well as Honan province, are grouped together as "Mandarin Cooking." This is a restaurant designation which suggests the food is "aristocratic," or "the best of its kind" since the Mandarins, the officials of the emperor's court, were the aristocrats of China.

Szechwanese cooking, the style of western China is peppery, fiery and stinging. The province itself is a vast fertile basin in the interior, bounded by craggy mountains and soaring cliffs that protect the region from the freezing winter winds of the north and the violent storms of the east. Its climate is hot, humid, semitropical. Since food there tended to spoil easily, spices were often used to preserve it. This led to a cuisine based on Szechwan peppercorns and chili peppers— red and green, fresh and dried. (They also helped the diner offset the debilitating effects of the weather.)

Szechwanese specialties include hot-and-sour soup and such seafood dishes as clams, lobster and shrimp prepared in a spicy hot sauce. Other favorites are paper-wrapped chicken, vegetables prepared in chicken fat, spicy steamed pork and a variety of mushrooms which appear both in vegetable dishes and in desserts.

The characteristic sharpness and sting of Szechwanese cooking is said to sensitize the palate to the many tastes and flavors that characterize the cuisine—salty, sour, sweet, bitter, fragrant and oily. Some say Szechwanese food is distinctly for the sophisticated palate; others believe it numbs the tastebuds. The Chinese themselves are a bit bewildered by the recent American interest in these fiery seasonings. One restaurateur observes, "Suddenly hot food is the fashion and the Chinese people don't know why."

Hunan province, southeast of Szechwan, shares the region's peppery preferences and its liberal use of spices and hot chili. Hunan is known for its many varieties of freshwater fish, its fish casseroles, its ham and twice-cooked pork.

THE TECHNIQUE OF ROASTING

Roasting—a method that has been used to cook meat and poultry ever since man discovered fire—calls for dry, indirect and intense heat to circulate slowly around the food, sealing in its flavor and most of its juices. The meat generally is elevated in some way so it doesn't stew in its own liquids. The Chinese vary this by marinating the meat first and by suspending it vertically in the oven.

The marinating is done with various mixtures of soy sauce, wine, chicken stock, honey, sugar, salt, pepper, garlic, scallions, fresh ginger root, vinegar, hoisin sauce, sesame paste, crushed chili peppers and other Chinese spices. (Sometimes red vegetable coloring is added to pork marinades.) Usually two or three hours of marinating are required, but longer periods may be used as well. (Never more than 10 or 12 hours; beyond that, the meat toughens.) The marinade is then drained and reserved for basting.

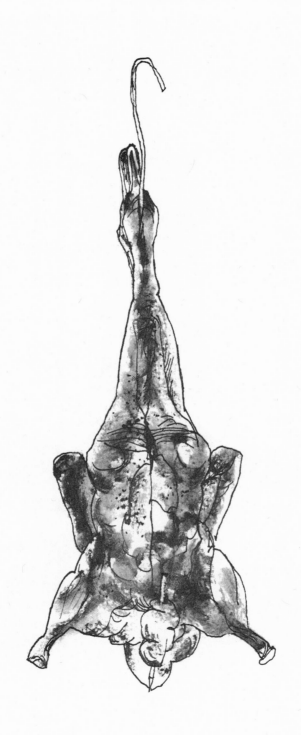

In vertical roasting, the meat browns evenly without the need for turning. Meanwhile the melting fat drips slowly off. Chinese restaurants and food shops use tall barbecue boxes or deep, pitlike ovens for roasting. They suspend whole poultry by the neck and either skewer the meat or hang it from hooks. Although most home ovens aren't lofty enough to suspend ducks and chickens in this manner, they are suitable for cooking spareribs and pork strips vertically.

The meat here is hung from a rack placed as high in the oven as possible. A roasting pan half-filled with water is then set on the oven floor to catch the drippings and keep them

from spattering and smoking. During roasting, the water is replenished as it evaporates. The drip pan itself may be lined with foil to further simplify cleanup.

Only one oven rack is needed. The meat is attached to it with metal hooks, which can be improvised from stainless-steel lacing pins, drapery hooks or large sturdy metal clips, bent with pliers to form S-shaped curves. The shorter end of the hook is inserted an inch or two from the edge of the meat, while the other end hooks onto the oven rack. Barbecued pork strips need only one hook each. A rack of spare-ribs needs six or more.

The meat is always hung as close to the center of the oven as possible. (Pork strips are spaced so they don't touch each other.) The drip pan is set directly underneath, with the meat hung high enough to clear the water in it.

While the oven preheats, the meat is attached. First, all the oven racks are removed; then one is placed on a work counter or table, extending far enough out so the meat can be conveniently hooked onto it. (The rack's opposite end is weighted down and stabilized with heavy books or a kettleful of water. Several layers of newspaper are placed on the floor below to catch the dripping of the marinade.) After the meat is hooked on securely, the metal rack is slid into place—high in the preheated oven.

The Chinese devised another ingenious way to roast when they found that salt could be made intensely hot over a small fire. They realized a quantity of salt could cook certain foods simply by transmitting its heat to them. Thus a whole chicken —snugly surrounded by hot salt—could be roasted with only enough additional heat to maintain the salt's temperature. When done, the tender, juicy chicken was surprisingly not salty at all. And the salt itself could be used again.

MODIFIED PEKING DUCK

1 duck (4 to 5 pounds)
Boiling water
1 tablespoon sherry

½ teaspoon salt
3 tablespoons honey
1 tablespoon soy sauce

1. Wash and dry the duck inside and out. Cut off and discard its bony wing tips.

2. Place duck in a large bowl or basin set in the sink. Pour the boiling water over both breast and back until the skin turns white. Drain. Cool with running water. Drain again. Pat dry with paper toweling.

3. Rub the sherry and salt into the body cavity. In a small bowl combine the honey, soy sauce and just enough heated water to thin the mixture slightly. Brush the mixture over the entire skin.

4. Suspend the duck in a cool, airy place, directing an electric fan at it for about an hour to dry the coating thoroughly. Meanwhile heat the oven to 325°F.

5. Set a rack in a roasting pan containing about 2 inches of water. Place duck on rack and roast 1¼ hours. (If any section browns too quickly, cover with foil.)

6. Turn bird over and roast about 30 minutes more. (The duck is done when its leg moves easily in the socket.)

7. Transfer bird to a cutting board. Let stand about 15 minutes. Then cut duck lengthwise in half with poultry shears

or a cleaver, then into rectangles about 2 inches square, each including both skin and meat.

8. Arrange these decoratively on a platter, skin-side up. Serve with Peking doilies, onion brushes and a hoisin dip. (Their recipes follow.)

NOTE: This adaptation of Peking Duck does not require that the bird's head and neck be intact.

PEKING DOILIES

2 cups all-purpose flour   *Flour*
1 cup boiling water   *Oil*

1. Put the flour in a heavy bowl. Make a well in the center and add the water gradually, stirring with a wooden spoon until the mixture acquires the consistency of cornmeal.

2. Lightly dust the hands and work surface with more flour, then knead the dough about 5 minutes until smooth and firm. Cover with a damp cloth. Let stand 30 minutes.

3. Knead the dough a few times more, then roll into a thin cylinder about 16 inches long and 1½ inches in diameter. Cut this cylinder crosswise into 1-inch disks.

4. Flatten each disk with the palm of the hand until it's about 4 inches in diameter and ¼ inch thick. Brush lightly with the oil on one side only. Then place one disk atop another—oiled surfaces touching—to form a double pancake. Gently press these together with the palm of the hand.

5. Lightly flour both the work surface and a rolling pin. Roll out each double pancake until it's about 6 inches in diameter and very thin. (For a perfectly round shape with even edges, roll from the center, rotating the disk one-quarter turn after each roll.)

6. When all the double pancakes have been rolled out, heat a small ungreased skillet over a medium flame. (The pan should be slightly larger in diameter than the pancakes, which are cooked one at a time.) Lightly brown each pancake, about a minute on each side. Immediately pull the two halves apart to separate.

7. When done, stack the individual doilies (there should be

12 to 16) on a preheated platter, keeping them covered with a damp cloth until all are done. Fold in quarters and serve warm.

NOTE: Peking doilies may be made in advance and refrigerated, then later reheated for 10 minutes in a slow oven or by brief resteaming.

ONION BRUSHES

16 *fairly thick scallions*   *Ice water*

1. Trim off the scallion roots and green tops, leaving the white stalks, which should be about 2½ inches long.

2. Notch both ends of each stalk by making several parallel cuts ½ inch deep, then make similar cuts crosswise to these.

3. Spread out cut ends with the fingers and place scallion stalks in a bowl. Add the ice water to cover. Refrigerate until the fringed ends curl like flower petals (about 2 hours). Drain well before serving.

HOISIN DIP

¼ cup hoisin sauce   1 tablespoon water
1 tablespoon soy sauce   1 teaspoon sugar
½ teaspoon sesame oil

1. In a small bowl, combine all ingredients, blending well.
2. Serve in dip dishes, allowing one dish for every two diners.

CANTONESE ROAST DUCK

1 duck (4 to 5 pounds)   1 tablespoon soy sauce
Salt   2 teaspoons sugar
1 garlic clove   4 cloves star anise
2 scallions   4 tablespoons honey
2 slices fresh ginger root   1 tablespoon vinegar
1 cup chicken stock   1 tablespoon soy sauce
2 tablespoons medium-dry   1 cup heated water
   sherry   Parsley

1. Have the duck at room temperature. Wash and dry the bird inside and out. Then lightly salt it inside and out. Meanwhile preheat the oven to 400°F.
2. Mince the garlic, scallions and ginger root. Combine these in a pan with the stock, sherry, soy sauce, sugar and star anise. Bring the mixture to a boil over medium heat, stirring frequently. Let cool 5 minutes.
3. Meanwhile sew up or skewer the duck's neck to make it completely leakproof. Place bird upside down in a large bowl or basin set in the sink. Ladle the seasoned liquid into the body cavity. Then sew up or skewer that cavity so that it, too, is leakproof.
4. Set a rack in a roasting pan containing about 2 inches of water. Place the duck, breast-side up, on the rack and roast 20 minutes. Meanwhile, in a bowl, blend the honey, vinegar, soy sauce and water.
5. Reduce oven heat to 325°F. and baste duck with the

honey mixture. Roast about 1½ hours more, basting with the mixture at 15-minute intervals. Turn bird once or twice for even browning, but do not use a fork, which would pierce the skin. (Wear rubber gloves instead.)

6. When duck is done—the leg will move easily in its socket—remove from the oven and place in a colander set in a bowl. Let stand about 15 minutes to cool slightly, then remove skewers from body cavity or snip the threads. Let the seasoned liquid drain into the bowl below.

7. Carve bird either Western or Chinese style. Arrange duck pieces on a serving dish, spooning the hot liquid over. Garnish with the parsley and serve.

NOTE: The duck may also be served cold without the gravy or combined with stir-fried vegetables or added to soups and noodle dishes.

The Chinese chop their birds, bones and all, into bite sized pieces meant to be eaten with chopsticks. The chopsticks are then used to remove the bones gracefully from the mouth. To carve poultry Chinese style: Lay the chicken or duck on a chopping block, breast-side up. With a cleaver, cut off the drumsticks and wings close to the body. Set these aside. Now chop the bird in half lengthwise down the center through the bone. Cut the breast sections away from the back and set them aside. Next, chop the back section in half lengthwise, then crosswise into one-inch sections. As each section is chopped, transfer it to an oval serving platter so the back is restored to its original form. Now chop off and discard the bony wing tips. Chop each wing crosswise into three roughly equal pieces. As these pieces are chopped, return each to its original location on either side of the bird's back in order to reconstruct the wing. Chop the knobby ends off the drumsticks and discard. Chop each drumstick crosswise into three roughly equal pieces. Position these on the platter as they are cut so that each leg is reconstructed and back in its original location on either side of the bird's back. Next, chop each half of the breast crosswise through the bone into one-inch sections. As these sections are chopped, arrange each, skin side up, on top of the back to reconstruct the shape of the breast. Garnish the bird with parsley. Serve hot or cold.

ROAST SOY CHICKEN

1 roasting chicken (3½ to 4 pounds)	2 whole scallions
3 cups water	2 slices fresh ginger root
1 cup soy sauce	1 tablespoon brown sugar
½ cup medium-dry sherry	1 teaspoon salt
	Dash of pepper

Lettuce

1. In a heavy saucepan—just about large enough to hold the chicken—put the water, soy sauce, sherry, scallions, ginger root, brown sugar, salt and pepper. Bring the liquids to a boil.

2. Meanwhile rinse the chicken and pat dry with paper toweling. Immerse bird in the soy mixture and bring to a boil again. Cover pan, reduce heat and simmer chicken about 30 minutes, turning it once to cook and color evenly. Meanwhile preheat the oven to 450°F.

3. Drain bird and put on a rack in a roasting pan containing about 2 inches of water. Roast until crisp and brown (about 15 minutes).

4. Let cool about 15 minutes so it can be handled. Then carve either Western or Chinese style. Arrange the pieces on a platter—over a bed of shredded lettuce—and serve.

SALT-ROASTED CHICKEN

1 chicken (3½ pounds)	½ teaspoon salt
5 pounds coarse salt	2 scallions
1½ tablespoons sherry	2 slices fresh ginger root

1. Select a heavy pot or casserole just large enough to hold the chicken. Pour the salt into the empty pot and heat over a medium flame until red hot, about 40 minutes, stirring from time to time to heat evenly and prevent scorching.

2. Meanwhile have the chicken at room temperature. Wash and dry it inside and out. Rub the body cavity lightly with the sherry and remaining salt.

3. Trim off the scallion roots and green tops and cut the stalks in 1-inch lengths. Place inside the body cavity with the ginger root. Truss chicken to make it as compact as possible.

4. When salt is intensely hot, transfer most of it temporarily to another pan, leaving a layer about 2 inches thick.

5. Place trussed bird breast-side down on this layer, then cover completely with remaining hot salt. Place lid on pot and cook over low heat for an hour.

6. Remove bird and brush off salt. Let cool slightly, then carve either Western or Chinese style.

BARBECUED SPARERIBS I

2½-pound rack of spareribs	*2 tablespoons sherry*
1 or 2 garlic cloves	*1 tablespoon honey*
2 scallions	*1 tablespoon brown sugar*
2 slices fresh ginger root	*1 tablespoon vinegar*
¼ cup soy sauce	*¼ cup tomato sauce*

1 teaspoon salt

1. Trim gristle and excess fat from the spareribs. Make slashes between each rib, about 1½ inches long, cutting these from the bottom.

2. Crush the garlic cloves slightly. Mince the scallions and ginger root. Place in a bowl along with the soy sauce, sherry, honey, brown sugar, vinegar, tomato sauce and salt. Blend well.

3. Place ribs in a flat, shallow, nonaluminum pan. (Cut them into two parts to fit, if necessary.) Brush mixture over both sides of the meat. Then pour the remainder over. Let ribs stand at room temperature about 2 hours, turning every 30 minutes to marinate evenly. Preheat the oven to 350°F.

4. Drain meat, reserving marinade. Hang the rib rack vertically in the oven over a drip pan containing about 2 inches of water. (Depending on the width of the spareribs and the width of the oven, the rack can be divided into several sections to fit.)

5. Roast until meat is done (about 1 hour), basting every 20 minutes with the marinade. (The ribs should be crisp, but not dry.) To test for doneness, cut into the thickest part of a rib. Cook a while longer if it's still pinkish.

6. Cut ribs apart and serve either hot or cold—plain or with dip dishes of plum sauce and hot mustard.

NOTE: The spareribs should be purchased with the rack intact and the bones neither cracked nor folded over. Also they may be roasted ahead and refrigerated, then brought to room temperature and reheated 5 minutes under a preheated broiler or over a charcoal grill.

BARBECUED SPARERIBS II

2½-pound rack of spareribs	1 garlic clove
1 teaspoon salt	½ cup pineapple juice
1 teaspoon sugar	¼ cup soy sauce
2 slices fresh ginger root	¼ cup medium-dry sherry

1 tablespoon brown sugar

1. Trim and slash the meat as in step 1 of the recipe above.
2. Rub with the salt and sugar. Let stand one hour.
3. Mince the ginger root and garlic clove. Combine in a bowl with the pineapple juice, soy sauce, sherry and sugar. Blend well.
4. Pick up steps 3, 4, 5 and 6 above.

BARBECUED PORK STRIPS

2 pounds boneless pork loin or butt	¼ cup medium-dry sherry
1 garlic clove	2 tablespoons brown sugar
1 scallion	2 tablespoons hoisin sauce
2 slices fresh ginger root	2 tablespoons honey
½ cup soy sauce	1 teaspoon salt
	Parsley

1. Trim off excess fat, then cut the pork with the grain into 6 separate strips, each measuring about 6 inches long, 2 inches wide and 1½ inches thick.

2. Crush the garlic slightly. Mince the scallion and ginger root. Place in a bowl along with the soy sauce, sherry, sugar, hoisin sauce, honey and salt. Blend well together.

3. Place pork strips side by side in a shallow dish or pan. Brush the mixture over and let stand at room temperature about 2 hours, turning meat from time to time to marinate evenly.

4. Meanwhile preheat the oven to 425°F. Drain pork, reserving marinade, and hang the strips vertically in the oven over a drip pan containing about 2 inches of water.

5. Roast 15 minutes. Reduce heat to 375°F. Baste with reserved marinade. Roast until done, about 40 minutes more, basting once or twice. (To check for doneness, cut the thickest strip in two. If it's still pinkish, cook a while longer.)

6. Cut each strip diagonally in ¼-inch slices. Arrange decoratively on a platter; garnish with parsley. Serve with dip dishes of plum sauce and hot mustard.

NOTE: Roast pork can be served alone as an appetizer, added to egg, fried rice and noodle dishes, or to stir-fried vegetables and soups.

CHINESE ROAST PORK

2 *pounds boneless pork loin*
1 *garlic clove*
1 *scallion stalk*
2 *slices fresh ginger root*
4 *tablespoons soy sauce*

3 *tablespoons medium-dry sherry*
1 *tablespoon brown sugar*
1 *tablespoon honey*
1 *teaspoon salt*

1. Have the pork trimmed of its excess fat and tied in a roll about 2½ inches in diameter.

2. Crush the garlic; mince the scallion and ginger root. Place in a bowl along with the soy sauce, sherry, sugar, honey and salt. Blend well together.

3. Place pork in a shallow dish. Brush on the mixture, then pour over the remainder. Let stand at room temperature about 2 hours, turning meat from time to time to marinate evenly.

4. Preheat the oven to 425°F. Drain pork, reserving marinade, and place on a rack in a roasting pan containing about 2 inches of water. Roast 15 minutes.

5. Reduce heat to 350°F. and baste with reserved marinade. Roast until done, about 45 minutes more, basting at 15-minute intervals.

6. Remove pork from oven and let stand about 15 minutes

to cool. Then cut in ¼-inch slices against the grain. Serve either hot or cold with a dip dish of hot mustard.

NOTE: Roasting pork with the bone in can be used, provided about 40 minutes of cooking time is allowed per pound in addition to the first 15 minutes at the higher temperature.

❀ *Steaming* ❀

OF THE MANY techniques the Chinese developed to cope with their fuel shortages, steaming is perhaps the most prudent. It requires only enough heat to boil water. The intense steam that water generates then circulates around the food and cooks it. And carrying this a step further, the Chinese devised a bamboo steamer that used the same heat and the same water to cook a number of dishes at once.

Steamed foods, although rarely seen on restaurant menus, are extremely popular in home cooking. Just about everything is steamed: meat, poultry, seafood and vegetables, even bread and pastry. The Chinese cook, it has been pointed out, can manage nicely without an oven but would surely be lost without a steamer.

Steamed foods have a number of advantages: They're always moist. Their natural freshness, flavor and nutrients can't boil away—the ingredients are never immersed directly in the water. (Seasonings are kept to a minimum to emphasize this freshness.) Oil isn't required, yet the food can't burn. The results are invariably light, highly digestible and generally lower in calories.

Steaming brings out the best in food, emphasizing the lightness and delicacy of chicken, tenderizing tough vegetables and cooking minced pork gently and evenly. Duck quickly sheds its fat, while eggs become custardlike and velvety.

Steamed fish is a great favorite. Its head and tail are always left intact for both aesthetic and practical reasons. A whole fish is more pleasing to the eye than a truncated one; the neck end doesn't overcook and the tender morsels in the cheeks and back of the head are retained and savored.

The fish to be steamed is cleaned and scaled, salted lightly inside and out, then marinated briefly and garnished. Usually the marinade is a wine–soy sauce combination to which vinegar, garlic and fresh ginger root may be added. Other seasonings might be fermented black beans or perhaps shrimp, hoisin or oyster sauce. The garnish might include any of the following, alone or in combination: shredded ham, pork, bacon, shrimp, mushrooms, scallions, etc. When the fish is steamed, its delicate blandness interacts wondrously with these flavorings.

Sometimes the Chinese will place the fish over two or three scallion stalks or slices of fresh ginger root. By creating a space between fish and dish, these flavorful props encourage a freer circulation of steam with the vapors passing below as well as above the food.

All sorts of fish are steamed: sea bass, striped bass, halibut, bluefish, mullet, perch, porgy, cod, pompano, mackerel, flounder, trout, etc. Most preferred are those varieties which flake readily when cooked and separate easily from the bone. (They're the simplest to eat with chopsticks.) A fish that weighs less than 2½ pounds is steamed whole; a larger one is cut first in thick slices or "steaks." Also steamed are virtually all varieties of seafood: clams, shrimp, lobsters, crabs.

Steaming is the traditional way of cooking "dim sum," the snack dishes especially favored by the Cantonese. "Dim sum" are buns and dumplings, both sweet and savory, served in small quantities at any hour of the day or night. Their daintiness, the Chinese say, touches the heart. Best known are the "shui mai," pouch-shaped dough coverings filled with flavorful mixtures of minced pork and shrimp and fluted prettily at the top.

Steaming may be the first step or the last in the preparation of a given dish. A duck, for example, might be steamed until done, then—for its final browning and crisping—briefly roasted or deep-fried. Or while a duck is browning, its stuffing can simmer separately. Subsequently, the bird is stuffed and steamed to a proper doneness.

Steaming is also used to keep food warm without loss of flavor or texture. It can reheat any meat or poultry, whether initially steamed or not. It can rewarm rice, freshen buns or noodles. Only seafood toughens with reheating and is better served cold the second time around.

Steaming has three simple requirements: a cooking vessel with a lid, a few inches of boiling water and a device to keep the food out of that water.

The special bamboo steamer that the Chinese devised—to be used in conjunction with a metal pot—fulfills these requirements nicely. The steamer itself consists of a series of circular trays which hold the food. These are stacked snugly in tiers, one atop the other, then set over a metal pot which holds the boiling water. As the steam vapors ascend vertically, they pass through the latticework bottom of each tray, encircling the food. Because the top tray is covered with a woven lid, the steam vapors are trapped and forced to recirculate again and again, thus cooking the food.

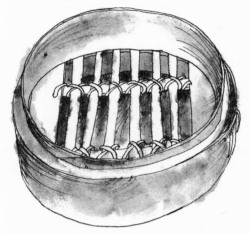

The metal pan is usually a Chinese wok, with the interlocking stack of bamboo trays sitting halfway down its semispherical sides. (Sometimes the trays are set over a wok in which rice is cooking. The steam rising from the rice—thus trapped—is forced to recirculate and cook the food above.) When a wok isn't available, a conventional pan can be used. Its diameter, however, must be a fraction of an inch smaller than the steamer so the trays can rest on its rim.

With a bamboo steamer, one can cook a number of the same or different foods. Thus meatballs might be on one layer, shrimp balls on another and stuffed vegetables on the third. (If the food generates liquids, it's set first on a small heatproof dish to prevent its dripping through the latticework onto the tray below.) Foods that require the most cooking are placed nearest the boiling water; those requiring the least are closer to the top.

Steaming trays range in diameter from eight to 24 inches. A 10-inch bamboo steamer, for example, is best with a 12-inch wok, while a 12-inch steamer will fit a 14-inch wok. The largest steamers are made of aluminum, not bamboo. Their trays are perforated, with the bottom-most unit holding the boiling water. As many as eight such trays can be accommodated at a time by Chinese restaurant stoves, which have high-powered gas units. Home stoves, with their smaller heat sources, can accommodate only two or three. Bamboo and aluminum units and lids of various sizes are sold in Chinese hardware and grocery stores.

Although special Chinese steamers are interesting to use, they're not essential. One can readily improvise a steaming device with the kitchen equipment on hand. The pan to hold the boiling water might be a round roaster, dutch oven, large stock pot or wok. It must be tall enough to contain at least two inches of water plus the food raised above it. Its lid must be snug enough to prevent the steam's escape but not so tight that excessive pressure builds up. (If such a lid is lacking, a double thickness of aluminum foil, pressed into place, can substitute.)

The rack device goes inside the pot and must be at least 2½ inches high to raise the food out of the water. For the steam to circulate properly, the diameter of the rack must be a bit smaller than that of the steaming vessel, while the height of the food must not interfere with the proper closing of the pan. Specifically, there should be at least half an inch between the rack and the sides of the pan and almost an inch of clearance between the top of the food and the lid.

Any of the following devices can serve: a three- or four-legged steaming rack standing about 2½ inches high; a cake-cooling rack or empty food can (with top and bottom removed) of similar height; a stack of saucers standing about 2½ inches tall; a heatproof bowl, coffee or custard cup, filled with water to keep it from floating (two cans or two cups offer even greater stability).

One can also duplicate the latticework function of the bamboo tray simply by setting a perforated rack—borrowed from a roaster or pressure cooker—over a can, cup or bowl. Or one can pierce a few holes in the bottom of a foil or metal pan.

The nature of the food to be cooked will determine if it's to be placed directly on the rack or tray or first in a dish or bowl. Individual ingredients such as meatballs, buns or stuffed vegetables can go directly on the rack. They are arranged in a single layer and spaced about half an inch apart to allow for expansion during cooking. Lining the rack with a double thickness of cheesecloth, predampened for greater absorbency, will keep such foods from sticking.

Soft and liquid-producing foods are set on heatproof dishes. The shallower the dish, the better, since more of the food is exposed to the moist, hot vapors. Although any heatproof dish can be used, nonmetallic ones, such as 10- or 12-inch Pyrex pie pans, are best.

Whole poultry and large coarse cuts of meat are steamed in deep, heatproof bowls. The bowl is set directly on the bottom of the steaming vessel, surrounded by boiling water to about two-thirds its height. The steaming pot is then covered with a lid. This variant, called bowl-in-a-pot or pot-in-a-pot steaming, cooks the food in two ways: indirectly with the boiling water and directly with the steaming vapors.

Bowl steaming can be used with cut-up ingredients as well. Pork cut in strips, for example, can be marinated in wine and other seasonings, then alternated with layers of dried and salted Chinese vegetables until the bowl is packed to the brim. After an hour or so of steaming, the meat is tenderized and the flavors blended. The excess liquids are then drained off and the bowl's contents neatly inverted onto a serving platter.

Depending on whether one cooks small stuffed mushrooms or large legs of pork, steaming time can range from a few minutes to several hours. A small fish, for example, needs about 15 minutes; a large one, 25.

When food is added to the steamer, the water should be at a rapid, vigorous boil. (In the case of bowl steaming, the water is first boiled in a ketttle, then carefully poured into the pot so it won't splash onto the food. This is easily done in a wok, which is wider at the top than the bottom.)

When the food is added, the heat is lowered to keep the boiling water from evaporating too quickly. (The water is never reduced to a simmer, however. The steam generated would be insufficient.) With long-cooking ingredients, the water must be checked at intervals. When it goes below the two-inch level, it's replenished with more of the same.

The steam that condenses inside the pan lid may present some dilution problems as it drips onto the food below. Some cooks lightly lay a sheet of wax paper over the food as protection. Such condensation is less of a problem with a wok; the moisture slides down the sloping sides of the lid and back into the boiling water. Such dripping is virtually no prob-

lem at all with bamboo steamers. Their condensation is minimal because bamboo retains the heat more efficiently.

Steaming is a placid technique. Once the food is in its
steaming dish, it needs no further attention—no rearranging
or last-minute embellishment. When done, it's brought directly to the table in the same dish.

The Chinese often retrieve shallow dishes from their steamers with a three-pronged metal lifter. This flexible device,
sold in Chinese hardware stores, can be adjusted to the diameter of the dish, provided that dish has a rim or lip. If a bowl
is to be retrieved, sturdy rubber gloves can be used instead
to protect the hands. (Pot holders don't do as well since they
can soak up some boiling water and become fiercely hot
themselves.)

A word of warning: after lifting the lid of the steamer—and
notwithstanding one's curiosity about the food's appearance
or aroma—one should let the scalding vapors disperse a second
or two before putting the face too close to the pot.

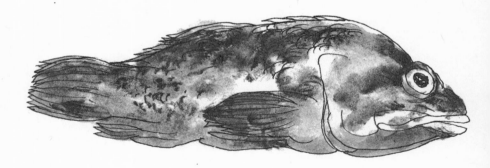

To sum up—when steaming on a bamboo rack: Arrange the
seasoned food on the latticework tray, lining it first with a
double thickness of predampened cheesecloth. Stack the trays
and cover the topmost one with a lid. Bring a few inches of
water to a boil in a wok or other suitable pan. Set the bamboo tiers over the boiling water. Reduce the heat and steam

until done. The food may be served in the bamboo tray itself, with a dinner plate set underneath to protect the table top.

When steaming on an improvised rack: Place the rack inside the pan. Add a few inches of water and bring to a rapid boil. Then set the seasoned food directly on the rack or in a shallow dish first. Cover the pan, reduce the heat and steam until done.

When steaming in a bowl: Put the seasoned food in a deep bowl and place the bowl on the floor of the steaming vessel. Bring water to a boil separately in a kettle. Pour it to about two-thirds the height of the bowl. Turn the heat on under the pan. Cover and steam until done.

STEAMED FISH WITH BLACK BEAN SAUCE

1 *fish* (1½ *to* 2 *pounds*)	2 *tablespoons soy sauce*
Salt	1 *tablespoon medium-dry*
2 *teaspoons fermented black*	*sherry*
beans	1 *tablespoon oil*
1 *garlic clove*	½ *teaspoon sugar*
2 *slices fresh ginger root*	1 *scallion*

1. Have the fish scaled and cleaned, with head and tail left intact. Rinse under cold running water; pat dry with paper toweling. Score on each side with several diagonal and parallel slashes, about ½ inch deep. Then sprinkle fish lightly with salt inside and out. Place on a shallow heatproof dish.

2. Meanwhile soak the black beans in water to cover for about 10 minutes; drain and squeeze out their excess moisture.

3. Crush the garlic, then mash to a paste with the soaked beans. Mince the ginger root and add to garlic-bean mixture, along with the soy sauce, sherry, oil and sugar, blending well. Brush mixture over top of fish.

4. Steam until done (about 20 minutes). Check for doneness in the thickest part at the back of the head. (The flesh should be white and opaque. If not, cook a few minutes longer.)

5. Shred the scallion; sprinkle over as a garnish and serve at once.

STEAMED SHERRY FISH

3 dried black mushrooms
1 fish (1½ to 2 pounds)
1 scallion
2 slices fresh ginger root
1 bamboo shoot

1 tablespoon sherry
2 tablespoons chicken stock
1 tablespoon sugar
1 tablespoon soy sauce
2 tablespoons vinegar

½ teaspoon salt

1. Soak the mushrooms in hot water to soften (about 30 minutes).
2. Have the fish scaled and cleaned with head and tail left intact. Rinse under cold running water; pat dry with paper toweling. Score on each side with several diagonal and parallel slashes, about ½ inch deep.
3. Cut the scallion stalk in 2-inch sections and place along with the ginger root inside the body cavity. Place fish on a shallow heatproof dish.
4. Stem and slice soaked mushrooms; slice the bamboo shoot. Arrange these around fish, then pour over the sherry and stock. Steam fish until done (about 20 minutes).
5. Meanwhile in a cup, combine the sugar, soy sauce, vinegar and salt, blending well. Serve with the fish as a dipping sauce.

STEAMED HARD-SHELLED CRABS

6 large or 12 small live crabs
4 slices fresh ginger root

4 tablespoons soy sauce
1½ teaspoons sugar

1. Place the live crabs in a sink filled with cold water. Let stand about 30 minutes to clean of sand and sediment. Then transfer with long-handled tongs to a large dish or bowl set in a steamer. Cover at once.
2. Steam until crabs turn bright red (about 20 minutes).

3. Meanwhile mince the ginger root. Combine and blend it with the soy sauce and sugar, then transfer to dip dishes.

4. Serve crabs with the dip, along with nutcrackers to break the shells.

STEAMED SHRIMP IN THEIR SHELLS

1 pound raw shrimp
Salted water to cover
2 slices fresh ginger root
½ teaspoon salt
1 tablespoon oil

1. Immerse the shrimp in the salted water for a few minutes to clean. Then with a knife or scissors, make a slit down the back but do not shell. Devein under cold running water.

2. Arrange shrimp in a shallow heatproof dish and sprinkle with the salt and oil. Shred the ginger root and sprinkle over.

3. Steam until shrimp turn pinkish (about 10 minutes). Cool, then refrigerate to chill. Serve cold, with or without their shells.

STEAMED MINCED PORK

1 pound boneless pork loin
   or butt
1 Chinese salt egg
½ teaspoon salt
½ teaspoon sugar
2 teaspoons cornstarch
1 tablespoon soy sauce
3 tablespoons chicken stock

1. Mince or grind the pork with some of its fat and place in a bowl.

2. Separate the salt egg. Reserve the yolk. Add the egg white to the bowl along with the salt, sugar, cornstarch, soy sauce and stock.

3. Blend mixture well by hand but do not overwork. Transfer to a shallow heatproof dish. With a fork, level meat to an even thickness.

4. Make a shallow depression in the center with a spoon. Place reserved egg yolk in it. Then steam until meat is cooked through and no longer pink (about 30 minutes). Serve hot.

STEAMED PEARL BALLS

½ *cup glutinous rice*
4 *dried black Chinese*
   mushrooms
1 *pound boneless pork loin*
   or butt
4 *water chestnuts*
1 *scallion stalk*

2 *slices fresh ginger root*
1 *tablespoon soy sauce*
2 *teaspoons medium-dry*
   sherry
1 *teaspoon cornstarch*
½ *teaspoon salt*
½ *teaspoon sugar*

1. Rinse the glutinous rice to remove some of the surface starch, then soak 4 hours in cold water to cover. Drain and spread on a towel to dry. Meanwhile soak the dried mushrooms in hot water to soften (about 30 minutes), then stem.

2. Mince or grind the pork, including some of its fat. Place in a bowl. Coarsely chop the water chestnuts and mushrooms and add.

3. Mince the scallion and ginger root and add to the bowl along with the soy sauce, sherry, cornstarch, salt and sugar. Blend well by hand but do not overwork mixture.

4. Form meat into walnut-sized balls, moistening the hands with water from time to time to keep the mixture from adhering.

5. Place glutinous rice on a dish or a sheet of waxed paper. Roll each meatball in rice to coat completely.

6. Arrange on a steamer tray lined with cheesecloth or on a heatproof dish. Steam until done (about 30 minutes). Serve hot.

STEAMED SPARERIBS WITH BLACK BEANS

1 tablespoon fermented
    black beans
2 pounds spareribs
1 garlic clove

1 tablespoon sherry
2 tablespoons soy sauce
½ teaspoon salt
½ teaspoon sugar

Parsley

1. Soak the fermented black beans in cold water to cover for about 10 minutes. Then drain and squeeze out their excess moisture.

2. Meanwhile cut the spareribs apart. With a cleaver, chop each rib crosswise in 1½-inch sections. Place in a bowl.

3. Crush the garlic, then mash to a paste with soaked beans. Add the sherry, soy sauce, salt and sugar, blending well.

4. Pour mixture over rib sections and toss to coat. Let stand one hour, turning meat occasionally.

5. Transfer meat to a shallow, heatproof dish. Steam until done (about 45 minutes). Garnish with the parsley and serve.

STEAMED GARLIC SPARERIBS

1 pound spareribs
1 garlic clove
2 slices fresh ginger root

1 tablespoon soy sauce
1 teaspoon cornstarch
Dash of pepper

1. Cut the spareribs apart. With a cleaver, chop each rib crosswise into ½-inch sections. Place in a bowl.

2. Mince the garlic and ginger root. Combine in a cup with the soy sauce, cornstarch and pepper, blending well. Add to spareribs, tossing to coat. Let stand about 30 minutes, turning meat occasionally.

3. Steam spareribs until done (about 30 minutes). Serve hot.

STEAMED BEEF AND MUSHROOMS

5 *dried black mushrooms* ½ *tablespoon sherry*
1 *pound flank steak* 1½ *teaspoons cornstarch*
1 *slice fresh ginger root* ½ *teaspoon salt*
1 *scallion* ½ *teaspoon sugar*
1 *tablespoon soy sauce* 1 *teaspoon oil*
1 *scallion*

1. Soak the mushrooms in hot water to soften (about 30 minutes).

2. Meanwhile cut the beef diagonally across the grain in ⅛-inch slices. Place in a bowl.

3. Mince the ginger root and first scallion. Combine in a cup with the soy sauce, sherry, cornstarch, salt and sugar, blending well. Add to beef, tossing to coat. Let stand 30 minutes, turning meat occasionally.

4. Transfer meat to a shallow heatproof dish. Squeeze excess liquid from mushrooms, then stem. Arrange mushroom caps over beef. Sprinkle the oil over. Then steam until meat is done (about 30 minutes).

5. Shred the remaining scallion. Sprinkle over as a garnish and serve.

STEAMED WHOLE SHERRY CHICKEN

1 *chicken (3 pounds)* ¼ *teaspoon sesame oil*
Salt 2 *scallion stalks*
2 *tablespoons sherry* 2 *slices fresh ginger root*

1. Wipe the chicken with moistened paper toweling. Sprinkle lightly with the salt inside and out.

2. Combine the sherry and sesame oil. Brush mixture over bird. Let stand about 30 minutes.

3. Cut scallion stalks in 2-inch lengths. Place these inside body cavity, along with the ginger root. Transfer chicken to a heatproof bowl, breast-side up.

4. Steam by the bowl-in-a-pot method until done (about 45 minutes). Carve Western or Chinese style. Serve hot or cold.

STEAMED CHICKEN WITH CHINESE SAUSAGES

1 chicken (2½ pounds)   *3 tablespoons sherry*
2 scallion stalks   *½ teaspoon salt*
2 slices fresh ginger root   *3 Chinese pork sausages*
1 tablespoon cornstarch   *3 tablespoons soy sauce*
              ½ teaspoon sesame oil

1. With a cleaver, chop the chicken—bones and all—into about 20 pieces: First quarter chicken, then chop each leg crosswise in three pieces and each wing, with the wing tip discarded, in two. Then chop the body crosswise through the breastbone into three pieces, dividing each into three roughly equal parts. Place chicken in a bowl.

2. Mince the scallion and ginger root. Then combine with the cornstarch, sherry and salt, blending well. Brush mixture over chicken. Let stand 30 minutes, turning pieces a few times.

3. Transfer chicken to a shallow heatproof dish and arrange skin-side up.

4. Rinse the Chinese sausages in warm water. Cut each diagonally into four parts and distribute decoratively over chicken. Steam until done (about 45 minutes).

5. Heat the soy sauce and sesame oil in a small saucepan, stirring. Pour over the dish and serve at once.

STEAMED GREEN ONION CHICKEN

1 *chicken (2½ pounds)*	1½ *tablespoons sherry*
2 *scallions*	3 *scallions*
2 *slices fresh ginger root*	2 *slices fresh ginger root*
½ *teaspoon salt*	4 *tablespoons oil*

1. Wipe the chicken with moistened paper toweling.

2. Mince the first scallions and ginger root. Combine in a cup with the salt and sherry.

3. Brush mixture over chicken inside and out. Let stand one hour at room temperature.

4. Place bird in a heatproof bowl and steam by the bowl-in-a-pot method until done (about 40 minutes). Let cool slightly.

5. With a cleaver, chop bird—bones and all—in bite-sized strips, about 1 by 2 inches. Arrange these on a preheated platter. Shred the remaining scallions and ginger root and sprinkle over the top.

6. Heat a wok or skillet. Add the oil and heat. Ladle it over

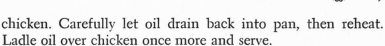

chicken. Carefully let oil drain back into pan, then reheat. Ladle oil over chicken once more and serve.

NOTE: In step 5, the chicken may be disjointed instead.

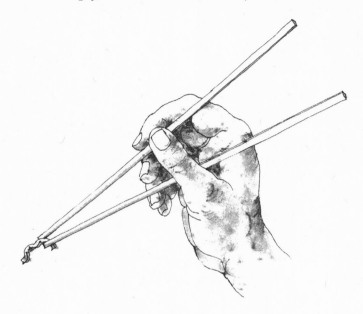

STEAMED STUFFED MUSHROOMS

12 *medium dried black mushrooms*

½ *pound boneless pork loin or butt*

¼ *pound fresh shrimp*

4 *to 6 water chestnuts*

1 *tablespoon medium-dry sherry*

2 *teaspoons cornstarch*

1 *teaspoon soy sauce*

½ *teaspoon salt*

Dash of white pepper

1. Soak the mushrooms in hot water to soften (about 30 minutes). Then stem.

2. Meanwhile mince or grind the pork with some of its fat. Place in a bowl.

3. Shell and devein the shrimp, then mince with the water

chestnuts. Add to pork along with the sherry, cornstarch, soy sauce, salt and pepper.

4. Blend the mixture well by hand but do not overwork. Divide in 12 parts to fill each mushroom cap.

5. Arrange mushrooms, stuffing-side up, on a cheesecloth-covered tray or lightly oiled heatproof dish. Steam until done (about 30 minutes). Serve hot or cold.

STEAMED EGGPLANT SALAD

1 *medium eggplant*	1 *tablespoon brown sugar*
1 *garlic clove*	1 *tablespoon vinegar*
2 *slices fresh ginger root*	1 *tablespoon oil*

½ *teaspoon salt*

1. Wash, but do not peel, the eggplant. Pierce its surface with a skewer or fork. Place eggplant on a rack and steam until soft (about 45 minutes).

2. Let cool so it can be handled, then stem and peel. Tear eggplant lengthwise and shred coarsely. Place in a bowl.

3. Mince the garlic and ginger root and add to eggplant along with the light brown sugar, vinegar, oil and salt. Toss to blend seasonings.

4. Cover the mixture and refrigerate several hours or overnight. Serve cold.

NOTE: For a finer texture, the eggplant may be chopped in step 2.

STEAMED EGGS AND CRABMEAT

½ *cup crabmeat*	1 *tablespoon oil*
6 *water chestnuts*	4 *eggs*
2 *scallions*	1 *teaspoon medium-dry*
¼ *teaspoon salt*	*sherry*
1 *teaspoon medium-dry*	¼ *teaspoon salt*
sherry	¼ *teaspoon sugar*

1 *cup chicken stock*

1. Flake the crabmeat, discarding the cartilage. Place in a bowl. Coarsely chop the water chestnuts and scallion stalks and add. (Reserve the green scallion tops for the garnish.)

2. Add the salt, sherry and oil to the mixture, blending well.

3. Break the eggs into another bowl. Add the remaining sherry, salt and the sugar. Stir gently only to blend yolks and whites.

4. Heat the stock almost, but not quite, to the boiling point. Add stock in a trickle to eggs, stirring slowly. Gently stir in the crabmeat.

5. Lightly oil a 10-inch Pyrex pie pan. Pour in the egg mixture. Steam over medium-low heat until it becomes custardlike

(about 30 minutes). Check with a toothpick for doneness. (It should emerge clean.)

6. Mince the scallion tops and sprinkle over as a garnish. Serve hot or cold.

NOTE: For a proper custardlike texture, the eggs must be stirred gently—not beaten—in step 3.

STEAMED SPONGE CAKE

4 *eggs*	½ *teaspoon vanilla extract*
¼ *cup cold water*	1 *cup flour*
1¼ *cups light brown sugar*	½ *teaspoon baking powder*

1. Separate the eggs. Beat the yolks and cold water, then gradually beat in the brown sugar and vanilla.

2. Sift the flour and baking powder; stir into yolk mixture.

3. Beat the egg whites until stiff but not dry. Fold in with a wooden spoon.

4. Lightly oil a cake pan 8 inches square and 2 inches deep. Pour in the batter. Rap pan sharply several times on a table top to remove air bubbles.

5. Steam until done (about 25 minutes). Check with a toothpick for doneness. (It should emerge clean.)

6. Remove cake from pan and let cool about 10 minutes. Then cut in small 2-inch squares. Serve warm.

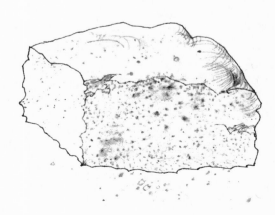

STEAMED HONEY PEARS

6 pears   *Chinese Five Spices*

Honey

1. Wash and stem the pears, then core, taking care not to cut through at the bottom. Set pears upright in a heatproof bowl.

2. Add a pinch of Five Spices to the cavity of each. Then fill with honey.

3. Steam until soft but not mushy (about 10 minutes). Serve warm.

NOTE: The pears for this dish should be ripe but still firm.

❀Braising and Stewing❀

OF THE VARIOUS Chinese seasonings, soy sauce is the most irreplaceable. It plays a role in every cooking technique, in every regional style. It is particularly essential in braising and stewing, both of which are slow-cooking methods.

Braising, the briefer of the two, is used with tender meats and poultry, with fish and fibrous vegetables. Stewing is applied to tougher cuts of meat and older poultry. It requires not only longer cooking but greater amounts of liquid as well. The liquid element in both, however, invariably includes soy sauce.

Soy sauce is made from soybeans, wheat, salt and yeast— fermented, then aged slowly and naturally. This dark, tangy liquid joins salt on the table as an ever-present condiment. In cooking, it enhances the flavor of meats, eggs, poultry, fish and vegetables. (It can make even the most unprepossessing cut of meat or poultry palatable.) And it's the predominant ingredient in many sauces, dips and marinades.

In smaller quantities, soy sauce heightens natural flavors. In larger ones, it blends with the ingredients. In either case, it unifies the various elements of the dish.

A good-quality, authentic soy sauce is vital for best results. Many grades and types are available. They range in color from light brown to nearly black and in density from delicately thin to thick and viscous.

The basic Chinese varieties are: (1) the thin or light

colored, (2) the dark and (3) the heavy. Thin soy—made with soybeans, flour, salt and sugar—is used where delicacy of flavor rather than intensity of color is desired. It enhances the taste of certain foods (white-meat chicken, seafood and some soups) without altering their characteristically light appearance.

Dark or black soy consists of the same ingredients as the light, plus caramel, which makes it considerably blacker and thicker. It's also aged a longer time. Dark soy gives foods and gravies a deeper, richer color, a more full-bodied flavor.

Heavy soy, being formulated with molasses, is the darkest and thickest of all, and somewhat bitter and viscous. It's used mainly for color and density in sweet-and-sour dishes.

Japanese soy is somewhere between the Chinese light and dark varieties. It tends to be less salty since it contains malt and large amounts of toasted wheat.

The most widely available, but least desirable, soys are the domestic varieties. Produced by a quick chemical process, these are highly concentrated, salty, bitter and extremely dark. They tend to stain rather than color the food and should be used sparingly, if at all.

Oriental soys are relatively inexpensive and even more economical when purchased in 21-ounce bottles. Buying them by the gallon proves more prudent still since they keep indefinitely without refrigeration.

BRAISING

For braising, only a small amount of soy and a cup or two of stock or water are required. The food is browned first in a little oil over medium-high heat. (This sears the outer surface and seals in the juices.) Then the stock or water, flavored with the soy and other seasonings, is added. This may be added all at once or in a sequence. For example, sherry, being more delicate, might be stirred in first so its flavor can be absorbed, then the soy sauce and the other flavorings. Those most frequently used here include scallions, garlic, ginger root, star anise, sugar and salt.

When all the liquids have been added and brought to a boil, the pot is covered, the heat reduced and the food slowly cooked until done. Just before serving, the gravy may be thickened with a cornstarch paste.

Peanut and other bland vegetable oils are used for the browning. (Lard is often used with vegetables and fish.) To permit proper browning, the cut-up meat or poultry is added to the skillet in batches, a pound or less at a time. The ingredients are usually not dredged first, although they should be quite dry when added. Fish, however, will receive a light dusting of flour or cornstarch to prevent its sticking to the pan.

Both the coarser and finer-fleshed varieties of fish lend themselves nicely to braising. Black bass, sea bass, carp, perch, porgy, trout, cod and fresh tuna are all suitable. Carp is particularly prized both as a delicacy and a good omen. Being plentiful in Chinese waters, it represents wealth and abundance. And because carp are said to swim in pairs, they symbolize connubial harmony and bliss as well. Traditionally a brace of carp, along with other gifts, is presented to the family of the bride-to-be.

In braising—as in steaming—smaller, more manageable fish are cooked whole, while larger ones are cut into thick slices or "steaks." If a fish is too large for a given pan, it can be divided into two or three sections, then reassembled when cooked.

The fish is rinsed with cold water, dried with paper toweling, lightly dusted with cornstarch or flour and browned. Browning can be done in two ways: The fish may be held over the pan

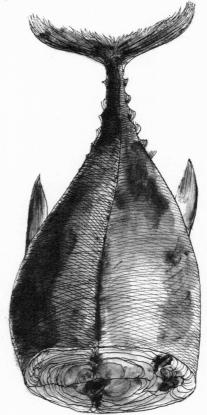

by its head and basted on all sides with hot oil. (Wearing stout rubber gloves is sensible here.) Or the fish may be held by the tail and lowered gently into the hot oil; the top and sides are basted while the bottom crisps. It is then carefully turned over and the process repeated.

In either case the fish, once browned, is immersed in the seasoned liquid and simmered about half an hour until done. Its skin is then rich and dark, while its meat is white, flaky and flavorful.

RED-STEWING

Stewing—the longer cooking method—is known as red-stewing because the soy sauce imparts a reddish-brown color to the food and its gravy. Here, larger coarser cuts of meat and poultry are slowly cooked in liquid to cover until they're tender enough to be pierced by fork or chopstick. The resulting dish is robust, mellow and richly concentrated.

Red-stewed dishes are extremely popular in home cooking but don't often appear on restaurant menus. (They tie up the burners of the stove too long.) Such slow-cooked dishes offer the home cook not only a rich blending of flavors and aromas, but great ease of preparation as well. Once in the pot, they need minimal attention. And, if necessary, they can be cooked in stages with the heat turned on and off at will.

Red-stewing, unlike braising, needs no initial browning or searing. It calls for the meat or poultry to be placed directly in a seasoned—usually preheated—cooking liquid. The liquid is then brought to a boil again, the pot covered and the heat reduced. The food is turned at intervals so that every part is immersed in the reddish-brown liquid, thus ensuring even cooking, flavoring and coloring.

Red-stewing is suitable for pork, including fresh ham, pork shoulder or butt, pork knuckles and pork trotters; for beef, including top round, boneless chuck and shanks of beef; for legs of lamb and for whole poultry. The meat is generally cooked whole or in large chunks. (It may be scored to cook faster and absorb more flavor.) On occasion, it's cut up to reduce the cooking time. Red-stewing is never used with fresh fish or seafood. It would damage their delicate taste and texture.

In China, slow-cooking was once done over charcoal in large earthenware pots. In contemporary kitchens, a wide variety of pans can be used if they're deep enough to hold the gravy, thick enough to keep the food from burning and have snug-fitting lids. The pan, for example, might be a dutch oven, an enameled cast-iron casserole or an oval roaster. The best pan for a given chicken, duck or cut of meat, however, is the one in which it fits comfortably and is surrounded by as much of the cooking liquid as possible.

The seasonings in red-stewing, as in braising, include sherry, ginger root, garlic, scallions, salt and star anise. Also cinnamon stick, Chinese Five Spices, dried tangerine peel, sesame oil, curry and vinegar. Other flavorings used here—in very small quantities to keep them subtle—are dried Chinese vegetables, such as lily buds and mushrooms and dried Chinese seafood, such as scallops, oysters and clams.

Sugar plays a strategic role in red-stewing—more to offset the predominant soy sauce than as a sweetener. Rock sugar is favored because it dissolves gradually, adding another dimension to the food while imparting a rich, shiny glaze. Rock sugar ranges in color from clear crystalline to pale amber and resembles small, uncut gems because of its irregular shapes. (Two three-quarter-inch lumps are the equivalent of two tablespoons of the granulated variety.)

Most seasonings are added at the beginning of braising and stewing, but sugar, if used in quantity—as it often is in red-

The Rolling-Cut ✿ 121

stewing—is not added until the last half hour of cooking (this is to keep it from scorching). When less than two tablespoons are called for, they're added at the same time as the other seasonings.

Both red-stewed and braised dishes may be extended by the addition of fresh vegetables, particularly the root varieties, such as carrots, turnips, potatoes, taro and lotus roots. Being fibrous, these are much improved by long, slow cooking. Other vegetables, such as cabbage, celery, string beans, broccoli, cauliflower, onions and fresh mushrooms, are also used. Since these require less cooking, they're added later. If they're done before the meat, they can be taken out of the pan and returned later for a brief reheating.

Tough, fibrous, cylindrical vegetables may be cubed, but they're usually sliced by the rolling-cut method, which converts them into fairly uniform, irregularly shaped wedges with a maximum of cooking surface. The vegetable here is cut into long diagonal slices and rolled or turned after each slice. This is done as follows: With the knife leaning slightly inward, a cut is made at a 30-degree angle, starting at the vegetable's root end. The vegetable is then rolled a quarter turn so that its cut surface faces upward. A second diagonal slice is made slightly above and partly across the first one, coming about halfway up the cut surface. (This gives the resulting wedge two long-pointed sides.) The cutting and rolling process continues, always in the same direction, until the cylindrical vegetable is completely sliced.

Another frequent red-stewing accompaniment is the gravy egg, excellent for snacks, hors d'oeuvres, buffets and picnics. The eggs are first fully hardboiled and shelled, then red-cooked in soy gravy about an hour more, either with or without the meat. To cook and color evenly, they're turned several times. When done, the eggs have reddish-brown exteriors and can be left whole, cut lengthwise in two, quartered or sliced. They're equally good served hot or cold.

Both braised and red-stewed dishes lend themselves to advance preparation. They keep about a week under refrigeration and their flavor improves after a day or two. Most can

be reheated. However, braised fish, like steamed fish, is best served cold the second time around.

Braised and stewed dishes are generally as good cold as they are hot. Their concentrated sauces jell easily and become delicious aspics. Beef or pork—chilled, sliced thin and arranged decoratively—is easy to prepare and serve. With its aspic spooned over, it provides the palate with a subtle experience of taste and texture. When garnished with parsley or minced scallions, it pleases the eye as well.

A classic chilled molded dish from northern China calls for a whole leg of lamb to be cooked in seasoned soy sauce, then cooled slightly and its gravy strained. Then the skin is separated from the tender meat, chopped fine and returned to the gravy to continue simmering until it virtually dissolves. The meat meanwhile is minced and transferred to a large mold.

The gravy, now further enriched and thickened, is strained once again, poured over the meat and the dish chilled. When the aspic sets, the congealed fat is discarded and the delectable jellied mound turned onto a serving platter where it's cut into slices and served.

The generous gravies, which red-stewed meats and poultry produce, are used in various ways. They're ladled over rice, noodles or precooked vegetables; they're used in stir-fried dishes as a rich substitute for stock or as a sauce for dipping.

The gravy may also be reserved as a master sauce to be used again and again in the cooking of other red-stewed meats and poultry. Such sauces were perpetuated two and three hundred years in China, passing from one generation to the next. At present, there's a master sauce in New York City nearly 15 years old and still going strong.

One begins a master sauce by cooking—but not seasoning too strongly—any red-stewed meat or poultry. The meat is eaten but the gravy is reserved. (It is then strained into a container through a double thickness of cheesecloth, covered and refrigerated. Its congealed fat is later discarded.) The gravy can be used again and again as a cooking medium for chicken, duck, pork, beef or lamb. (Fish, seafood and strongly flavored ingredients are never cooked in it, however. They would damage its subtlety.)

With a quart or so of master sauce and some fresh meat or poultry, preparing a red-stewed dish is simplicity itself. The sauce is brought to a boil in a deep, heavy pot, the meat added and the liquid brought to a boil again. The pot is covered, the heat immediately reduced and the meat simmered until tender. The end result is juicy, tender and rich brown in color. Like other red-stewed dishes, it's equally good served hot or cold.

The master sauce itself is never eaten but always reserved for future use. It must be replenished on occasion with such ingredients as soy sauce, sherry, scallions, ginger root, salt and sugar. Thus, after a use or two, a quarter cup each of soy sauce and sherry will be added along with a scallion, a few slices of fresh ginger root, a pinch of sugar and salt. Occasionally, one might add a clove or two of star anise, a few Szechwan peppercorns, or a pinch of Chinese Five Spices.

A master sauce can be kept "alive" indefinitely if strained and refrigerated each time and used either for cooking at least once a week or else brought to a boil. If it's to be used at longer intervals, it can be frozen, then reheated without advance thawing.

The more frequently meat and poultry are cooked in a master sauce, the more it takes on their juices, flavors and aromas and the more subtly complex it becomes. Outwardly it is transformed into an aspic—rich, dense and mahogany-colored.

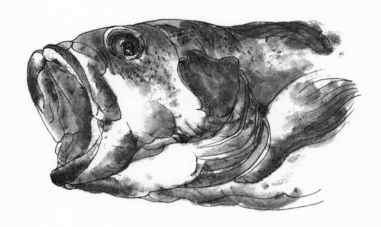

BRAISED FISH

1 *carp or sea bass (about*	1½ *tablespoons sherry*
2 *pounds)*	1 *teaspoon brown sugar*
Salt	3 *tablespoons oil*
1 *tablespoon flour*	2 *to 3 cakes fresh bean curd*
¾ *cup chicken stock*	2 *teaspoons cornstarch*
3 *tablespoons soy sauce*	2 *tablespoons cold water*

Parsley

1. Have the fish scaled and cleaned, with head and tail left intact. Rinse with cold running water. Pat as dry as possible with paper toweling.

2. Score fish on each side with several diagonal slashes about ½ inch deep. Sprinkle lightly with the salt inside and out. Then sprinkle the flour evenly over the skin.

3. Gently heat the stock in a small saucepan. In a cup combine the soy sauce, sherry and brown sugar.

4. Heat a long oval roasting pan on top of the stove. Add the oil and heat; then add fish. Carefully brown over medium-high heat (about 3 minutes on each side).

5. Stir in the soy-sherry mixture for about a minute, then the heated stock. Bring liquids quickly to a boil. Cover pan, reduce heat to medium-low and cook 10 minutes.

6. Cut the bean-curd cakes in 1-inch cubes and add. Cook covered until fish is done (about 7 minutes more).

7. Transfer fish carefully in one piece to a preheated serving platter. Arrange bean curd around it.

8. Blend the cornstarch and cold water to a paste. Stir into pan liquids over medium heat to thicken. Then spoon sauce over fish. Garnish with the parsley and serve.

BRAISED PORK AND CARROTS

2 pounds boneless pork
6 carrots
1 scallion stalk
2 slices fresh ginger root
1½ cups chicken stock

4 tablespoons oil
¼ cup soy sauce
2 tablespoons medium-dry
  sherry
½ teaspoon salt

2 tablespoons rock sugar

1. Cut the pork in 1-inch cubes. Peel or scrape the carrots and slice by the rolling-cut method. Cut the scallion in 1-inch lengths; shred the ginger root. Gently heat the stock. Slowly preheat a deep, heavy pan on top of the stove.

2. Heat a wok or skillet. Add the oil and heat. Add pork cubes and brown over medium-high heat on all sides. Add scallion and ginger root. Stir-fry about a minute to brown lightly. Then transfer meat and other stir-fried ingredients to the preheated pan.

3. Add the soy sauce, sherry and salt. Cook a minute or two, tossing meat to blend flavors. Then add heated stock.

4. Quickly bring liquids to a boil. Cover pan, reduce heat to low and simmer 30 minutes, turning meat once or twice.

5. Add sliced carrots along with the rock sugar and continue simmering covered until pork is cooked through (about 30 minutes more), turning meat occasionally. Spoon some of the sauce over and serve.

STEWED PORK IN BROWN SAUCE

2 to 3 pounds boned pork shoulder	1 cup soy sauce
8 scallions	2 cups water
½ cup medium-dry sherry	2 star anise
	½ cup brown sugar

1. Cut the pork with its rind in 1½-inch squares. Trim the scallions but leave them whole.

2. Arrange scallions on the bottom of a thick, heavy pan and place pork squares on top, skin side up.

3. Add the sherry, soy sauce, water and star anise and bring quickly to a boil. Then cover pan, reduce heat and simmer 30 minutes.

4. Add the sugar and simmer, covered, 30 minutes more, turning meat occasionally.

5. Arrange scallions on a serving platter with pork squares on top. Spoon some of the sauce over and serve.

RED-STEWED PORK SHOULDER

Pork shoulder roast (about
  3 pounds)
1 garlic clove
2 tablespoons soy sauce
2 tablespoons medium-dry
  sherry

½ cup soy sauce
¼ cup medium-dry sherry
1 teaspoon salt
2 slices fresh ginger root
2 cups water
2 tablespoons rock sugar

1 scallion

1. Wipe the pork with moistened paper toweling. Cut the garlic clove in half and rub over meat.

2. Combine the soy sauce and sherry. Brush mixture over pork. Let stand 2 hours at room temperature; then transfer meat to a deep, heavy pot.

3. Add the remaining soy sauce and sherry along with the salt and ginger root and heat, stirring. Meanwhile heat the water.

4. Stir in the hot water and quickly bring the liquids to a boil. Cover pan, reduce heat to low and simmer 1½ hours, turning meat at 20-minute intervals to cook evenly.

5. Add the rock sugar and simmer pork until done (about 30 minutes more), turning meat once or twice.

6. Let pork stand covered until cool, then refrigerate to chill.

7. Slice meat thin against the grain and arrange on a serving platter. Mince the green scallion tops, sprinkle over as a garnish and serve.

TWICE-COOKED SZECHWANESE PORK

2 pounds pork tenderloin
3 cups water
1 garlic clove
1 scallion

2 slices ginger root
2 tablespoons oil
½ teaspoon salt
1 tablespoon soy sauce

½ teaspoon Tabasco sauce

1. Put the pork in a saucepan, add the water and bring quickly to a boil. Cover pan, reduce heat to low and simmer

until pork is cooked through (about an hour). Remove from pan and let cool. (Reserve the liquid for stock.)

2. Cut pork in ¼-inch-thick slices, then cut each slice in two. Crush the garlic clove slightly. Cut the scallion in ½-inch sections. Slice the ginger root.

3. Heat a wok or skillet. Add the oil and heat. Add the salt, then garlic and scallions. Stir-fry a few times.

4. Add the meat slices and ginger root. Sprinkle meat with the soy sauce and Tabasco. Gently stir-fry to heat, color the pork evenly and blend the flavors (about 5 minutes), then serve.

LION'S HEAD

4 dried black Chinese mushrooms	½ teaspoon salt
	½ teaspoon sugar
1 pound boneless pork	1 egg
6 water chestnuts	4 tablespoons oil
2 scallions	1 cup chicken stock
2 slices fresh ginger root	2 tablespoons soy sauce
1 tablespoon soy sauce	1 pound fresh spinach
1½ tablespoons medium-dry sherry	2 tablespoons oil
	½ teaspoon salt

1. Soak the mushrooms in hot water to soften (about 30 minutes).

2. Meanwhile mince or grind the pork with some of its fat and transfer to a bowl. Mince the water chestnuts, scallions and ginger root; add to meat.

3. Squeeze soaked mushrooms to remove their excess liquid. Discard stems and mince caps. Add these to meat along with the soy sauce, sherry, salt and sugar. Lightly beat the egg and add.

4. Blend the ingredients by hand but do not overwork mixture. Divide into four equal parts, shaping each into a large meatball.

5. Heat a wok or skillet. Add the oil and heat. Add meatballs and brown on all sides over medium-high heat.

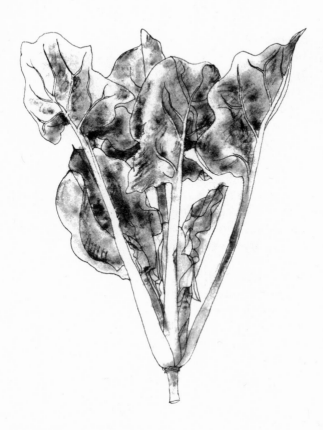

6. Heat the stock and remaining soy sauce in a deep, heavy pan. Add meat and quickly bring liquids to a boil. Cover pan, reduce heat and simmer 35 minutes, carefully turning meatballs once or twice. Meanwhile remove tough ends of the spinach, wash and drain.

7. Wash and reheat wok or skillet. Add the remaining oil, stir in the remaining salt, then add spinach. Stir-fry only to soften (about 2 minutes).

8. Arrange spinach over meatballs. Cover and cook until pork is no longer pink (about 10 minutes more). Transfer spinach to a preheated serving platter with the meatballs on top. Spoon some of the sauce over and serve.

BRAISED CUBED BEEF

2 *pounds boneless beef*	2 *cups chicken stock*
1 *scallion*	3 *tablespoons oil*
2 *slices fresh ginger root*	½ *cup soy sauce*
1 *garlic clove*	¼ *cup medium-dry sherry*

1 *tablespoon sugar*

1. Cut the beef in 1½-inch cubes. Cut the scallion in 1-inch sections. Slightly crush the ginger root and garlic clove. Gently heat the stock in a small saucepan.

2. Heat a wok or skillet. Add the oil and heat. Add beef cubes and brown on all sides over medium-high heat. Add garlic, scallion and ginger root, stir-frying to brown lightly. (Add more oil if necessary.) Meanwhile preheat a deep, heavy pan.

3. Transfer meat and browned ingredients to preheated pan. Stir in the soy sauce and cook a minute or two. Stir in the sherry and sugar to heat. Then add warmed stock.

4. Bring the liquids quickly to a boil. Cover pan and reduce heat. Simmer until beef is done (about 1 hour).

AROMATIC SPICED BEEF

1 *whole beef shin*	4 *to 6 cloves star anise*
1 *cup soy sauce*	1½ *tablespoons brown sugar*
½ *cup medium-dry sherry*	1 *teaspoon salt*
3 *cups water*	1 *garlic clove*

1 *scallion*

1. Have bone removed from the beef shin, then trim off the fat and membrane. Place meat in a deep, heavy pan.

2. Add the soy sauce, sherry, water, star anise, sugar and salt. Crush the garlic slightly and add.

3. Bring the liquids quickly to a boil. Then cover pan, reduce heat to low and simmer beef until fork tender (about 3 hours), turning it at 30-minute intervals.

4. Let meat cool in the covered pan. Then strain the sauce

through a double thickness of cheesecloth. Refrigerate meat
—but not sauce—to chill.

5. Cut chilled beef against the grain in thin slices. Arrange
on a serving platter with some of the sauce spooned over.
Cover and chill again until sauce jells (about an hour).
Mince the green scallion tops, sprinkle over as a garnish and
serve.

NOTE: For the shin, substitute 3 pounds of beef chuck or
eyeround, rolled and tied.

RED-STEWED LAMB

2 pounds leg of lamb	*3 slices fresh ginger root*
Water to cover	*½ cup soy sauce*
3 scallions	*1 teaspoon salt*

1. Wipe the lamb with moistened paper toweling, then cut
in 1-inch cubes. Place in a deep, heavy pan. Add water and
bring quickly to a boil.

2. Meanwhile cut the scallions in 1-inch lengths; slice the
ginger root. Then add these along with the soy sauce and salt.

3. Cover pan and reduce heat. Simmer until meat is done,
about 2 hours.

NOTE: Should too much liquid evaporate during cooking, it
may be replenished as necessary with preheated chicken stock.

BRAISED CHICKEN AND CHESTNUTS

½ pound dried chestnuts	*4 tablespoons oil*
3 cups water	*½ cup soy sauce*
1 chicken (3 pounds)	*1½ tablespoons medium-dry*
2 whole scallions	*sherry*
1 garlic clove	*1½ cups chicken stock*
2 slices fresh ginger root	*1 teaspoon brown sugar*
½ teaspoon salt	

1. Boil the dried chestnuts in the water for 1 hour. Let
cool slightly and remove their outer membranes.

2. Wipe the chicken with moistened paper toweling. Then with a cleaver, chop bird—bones and all—into 2-inch sections. Dry well with paper toweling. Cut the scallions in 1-inch lengths. Slightly crush the garlic and ginger root.

3. Heat a wok or skillet. Add the oil and heat. Add the scallions, garlic and ginger root, stir-frying to brown lightly. Remove these from pan and reserve.

4. Add chicken pieces in two or more batches and brown lightly on all sides over medium-high heat. (Add more oil as necessary.)

5. Meanwhile in a deep, heavy pot, heat the soy sauce, sherry, stock, sugar and salt. Then add chicken and other browned ingredients and bring liquids quickly to a boil. Cover pan, reduce heat to medium and cook 10 minutes.

6. Add chestnuts and cover pan again. Reduce heat to low and simmer until chicken is done (about 30 minutes).

7. Arrange cooked chicken and chestnuts on a preheated serving dish. Spoon some of the sauce over and serve.

NOTE: For the dried chestnuts, substitute a comparable amount of peeled fresh chestnuts, but omit step 1.

SOY CHICKEN

1 *chicken (3 pounds)*	3 *tablespoons medium-dry*
Salt	*sherry*
2 *scallions*	2 *slices fresh ginger root*
1½ *cups soy sauce*	2 *to 3 small lumps rock sugar*
3 *cups chicken stock*	*Sesame oil*

Parsley

1. Wipe the chicken with moistened paper toweling. Sprinkle its body cavity lightly with salt. Cut the scallions in 2-inch lengths.

2. In a deep, heavy pot, combine and blend the soy sauce, stock, sherry, scallion and ginger root. Bring the liquids quickly to a boil, then add chicken.

3. Bring to a boil again, cover pan, reduce heat to medium-low and simmer 15 minutes. Then turn bird over.

4. Add the rock sugar. Simmer until chicken is done (about 30 minutes more), turning it once or twice for even cooking and coloring. Remove bird from pan and let cool.

5. Lightly brush its skin with the sesame oil. Then with a cleaver, chop the bird—bones and all—in 2-inch sections or carve Western style.

6. Serve chicken at room temperature, garnished with the parsley.

SPICED CHICKEN LIVERS

1 *cup soy sauce*	1 *tablespoon sherry*
2 *cups water*	½ *cinnamon stick*
1½ *tablespoons rock sugar*	2 *star anise*

1 *pound chicken livers*

1. In a saucepan, combine the soy sauce, water, sugar, sherry, cinnamon and star anise. Bring quickly to a boil, then simmer covered 30 minutes to blend flavors.

2. Meanwhile trim the fat and gristle from the chicken livers. Add livers to pan. Quickly bring liquids to a boil again. Cover pan, reduce heat to low and simmer 30 minutes more. Serve hot or cold.

RED-STEWED DUCK

6 *dried black Chinese*   4 *tablespoons medium-dry*
  mushrooms   *sherry*
1 *duck (4 pounds)*   1 *teaspoon sugar*
Boiling water   ½ *teaspoon salt*
4 *scallions*   2 *slices fresh ginger root*
½ *cup soy sauce*   1 *cup bamboo shoots*
                  Cold water

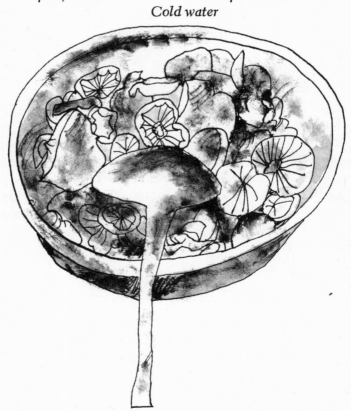

1. Soak the dried mushrooms in hot water to soften (about 30 minutes).

2. Immerse the duck in a large pot of boiling water and parboil 10 minutes over high heat. Drain duck, discarding water, and rinse bird with cold running water.

3. Cut the scallions in 2-inch lengths. Place them inside duck cavity. Then transfer bird, breast-side down, to a deep, heavy pan. Add the soy sauce, sherry, sugar and salt.

4. Stem soaked mushrooms and add to pan along with their soaking water. Slice the ginger root and bamboo shoots and also add.

5. Add enough fresh cold water to pan to cover duck. Bring the liquids quickly to a boil. Cover pan, reduce heat to low and simmer 1 hour.

6. Turn duck, breast-side up, and simmer covered until done (about 45 minutes more).

7. Let cool slightly. With a cleaver, chop bird—bones and all—in 2-inch sections or carve Western style. Then serve.

BRAISED ONION DUCK

1 duck (4 pounds)	5 cups water
1 pound white onions	1 tablespoon brown sugar
2 tablespoons soy sauce	2 tablespoons medium-dry
2 tablespoons oil	sherry
4 tablespoons soy sauce	

1. Wipe the duck with moistened paper toweling; then pat dry.

2. Thickly slice the onions. Brush the soy sauce inside the body cavity, then stuff cavity with onions.

3. Heat a wok or skillet. Add the oil and heat. Gently brown duck on all sides over medium heat (about 10 minutes). Transfer bird, breast-side down, to a thick, heavy pan.

4. Add the water, sugar, sherry and remaining soy sauce. Bring the liquids quickly to a boil. Then cover pan, reduce heat to low and simmer 1 hour. Turn duck over and simmer until done, about 30 minutes more.

5. Let cool slightly. With a cleaver, chop bird—bones and all—in 2-inch sections or carve Western style. Then serve.

BRAISED DUCK WITH PINEAPPLE

1 duck (4 pounds)
2 slices fresh ginger root
1 tablespoon sugar
2 tablespoons medium-dry
  sherry
2 tablespoons soy sauce
½ teaspoon salt

1 garlic clove
5 tablespoons oil
3 cups water
½ cup pineapple juice
2 tablespoons soy sauce
4 slices canned pineapple
1 tablespoon cornstarch

3 tablespoons water

1. Wipe the duck with moistened paper toweling. Mince the ginger root and combine in a cup with the sugar, sherry, soy sauce and salt. Blend the mixture well, then brush over duck.

2. Crush the garlic clove slightly. Heat a wok or large pan. Add the oil and heat. Add duck and brown on all sides over medium heat; then transfer bird, breast-side down, to a deep, heavy pan.

3. Add the water, pineapple juice and remaining soy sauce. Bring quickly to a boil. Cover pan, reduce heat to low and simmer about 1½ hours, turning duck occasionally for even cooking.

4. Transfer bird to a preheated serving platter. Cut each pineapple slice in four parts and arrange over duck.

5. In a cup, blend the cornstarch and water to a paste. Add to pan liquids and stir in to thicken over medium-high heat. Pour sauce over duck and serve.

BRAISED EGGPLANT

1 *large eggplant*	3 *tablespoons oil*
Salt	2 *tablespoons oil*
3 *tomatoes*	¼ *cup soy sauce*
2 *onions*	½ *cup chicken stock*
1 *garlic clove*	1 *teaspoon sugar*
2 *slices fresh ginger root*	½ *teaspoon salt*

Dash of pepper

1. Peel the eggplant and cut in 1½-inch slices. Sprinkle liberally with the salt and let stand 1 hour. Then drain eggplant, pat dry with paper toweling and cut in 1½-inch cubes.

2. Plunge each tomato into boiling water for 20 seconds, then peel each immediately and cut in wedges. Cut the onions in similar wedges. Crush the garlic clove and ginger root slightly.

3. Heat a wok or skillet. Add the first oil and heat. Add eggplant cubes. Brown quickly over medium-high heat, then remove from pan.

4. Add the remaining oil and heat. Add and lightly brown the garlic, ginger root and onions. Meanwhile in a deep, heavy pan, combine the soy sauce, stock and sugar.

5. Bring the soy mixture to a boil. Add eggplant and other browned ingredients along with the remaining salt and pepper. Cover pan, reduce heat to medium-low and cook eggplant until nearly done (about 15 minutes). Add tomato wedges. Cook 5 minutes more and serve.

BRAISED BLACK MUSHROOMS

¼ *pound dried black*
  mushrooms
2 *tablespoons sugar*

2 *tablespoons soy sauce*
1 *tablespoon sesame oil*
2 *tablespoons oil*

1. Soak the dried mushrooms in hot water to soften (about 30 minutes). Squeeze out excess liquid, reserving this and the soaking water itself, then stem mushrooms.

2. Add enough fresh cold water to the soaking liquid to make 1½ cups, then stir in the sugar, soy sauce and sesame oil, blending well.

3. Heat a wok or skillet. Add the oil and heat. Add mushroom caps and stir-fry gently to brown.

4. Stir in the soy mixture and bring quickly to a boil. Reduce heat and simmer, covered, until most of the liquid is absorbed (about 30 minutes), stirring occasionally toward the end. Serve hot or cold.

NOTE: These can be served alone as a side dish or added whole or cut-up to other dishes.

Firepot Cooking and Other Simmering

SIMMERING, the simplest method of all, calls for the raw ingredients to be cooked directly in a bubbling liquid, usually water. As they cook, they flavor and enrich that liquid.

Soups are made by simmering. So are "pure stewed" dishes, which produce crystal-clear broths. Congee, a creamy rice dish, is simmered, as is the festive and majestic firepot.

THE FIREPOT

The firepot, served between November and March, is an elegant one-dish meal in which the diners cook their own food at the table in a constantly simmering broth.

Although festive now, the firepot's origins were humble. Some say it was introduced in the thirteenth century when nomadic Mongol tribes were overrunning northern China. These conquering Moslems—who shunned pork and favored lamb—liked to spear thick slivers of mutton and plunge them into great cauldrons of boiling water. They seasoned the cooked meat pungently, gobbled it down and finished off the meal with mouthfuls of the hot liquid, which by then had become a zesty, rich soup.

Others believe the firepot goes back to a northern home-heating method which called for large pots of burning charcoal. Perhaps someone warming himself on a cold winter's day speculated: Why not let the charcoal heat some water? And while that water is boiling, why not use it for cooking?

At any rate, the Chinese developed a special pot to hold both the charcoal and the water. Raw ingredients, cut in bite-sized pieces, were dropped into the bubbling liquid, where they cooked rapidly. And while the charcoal warmed the outer man, the food and broth gave comfort to the inner one.

The firepot, still fueled by charcoal, continues to play a convivial role when family and friends gather. Although not directly associated with any Chinese holiday, it appears frequently during the time of the Chinese New Year. The holiday itself is celebrated on the first day of the lunar calendar —in late January or early February. This major event of the year marks both an end and a beginning: winter is almost over; a new agricultural cycle is about to begin. There is great rejoicing and optimism as one watches the old year depart and looks forward to the promise and prosperity the new year might bring.

The next major holiday is the Dragon Boat Festival, which takes place in late June or July when hope is expressed for enough rain to sustain the crops. Taking place on the fifth day of the fifth lunar month, it is also regarded as a time of potential evil when malevolent spirits must be warded off. The superstitious wear amulets on this day to protect them from harm. They're also careful to avoid lizards, centipedes, scorpions and toads.

This observance gets its name from the dragon boat races held to commemorate the untimely death of Chu Yuan, statesman, scholar and poet, who lived about 300 B.C. Chu Yuan was greatly upset when the Emperor—who had fallen in with evil advisers—began to spend lavishly and tax his people unmercifully. To protest this corruption, Chu Yuan threw himself into the river. Learning of this, the villagers set out in dragon-shaped boats to find him. But they never did. To appease his spirit, they scattered rice dumplings on the water —enclosing them in bamboo leaves so the fish could not get at them. Every year, on the fifth day of the fifth lunar month, the Chinese still eat such dumplings in memory of the good Chu Yuan.

The last major observance—and second in importance to the New Year event—is the Moon Festival, celebrated in late

August or early September when fruits and vegetables are harvested for winter storage. This is the time for giving thanks to the deities of earth, wind and rain for their assistance with the crops. On that fifteenth day of the eighth lunar month, with the moon at its fullest, roundest and brightest for the year, families gather 'round tables laden with fruit, wine and moon cakes. (The roundness of the cakes symbolizes fulfillment and completeness.) Legends are told then of the lady who stole the pill of longevity and was forced to flee to a palace on the moon. It is said on that night that her silhouette can be seen clearly on the moon.

The firepot, although celebrating no specific holiday, inevitably creates its own festive feeling. The diners who gather

'round—to share the broth and its contents—respond to a happy combination of individuality and togetherness. Each chooses the ingredients he wishes in the quantity he wants, then cooks and seasons these to his taste. No previous experience is needed. Everyone becomes an expert quickly.

The ingredients cooked in the firepot vary from region to region. Meat predominates in the north. In the south seafood is more widely used. At one extreme is the Mongolian hotpot, which features lamb exclusively. (It is accompanied by leeks, garlic, strong condiment sauces and either wheat-flour noodles or steamed buns.) At the other extreme is the fish and seafood firepot of Fukien, accompanied by watercress and rice-flour noodles. In between are many others offering a varied sampling of meat, fish and poultry, accompanied by Chinese cabbage, spinach and peastarch noodles.

Despite these regional differences, all firepots follow a basic cooking pattern. Six to eight diners are seated at a table, preferably a round one. At the center is the liquid-filled vessel; arranged around it are various platters of raw ingredients, cut in convenient bite-sized pieces, along with smaller dishes of condiments.

The diner, choosing a morsel or two at a time, picks it up with chopsticks, dips it into the simmering liquid, withdraws it when cooked, seasons it to his taste and consumes it at once.

When the cut-up ingredients have been eaten—or when the diners have had their fill—noodles and vegetables are added to the now subtle and savory broth. When these, too, have been consumed, the well-flavored liquid serves as the satisfying grand finale of the meal. No other beverage is offered and no dessert, although fruit is sometimes served.

The firepot itself, sometimes called a Peking Hotpot, is a handsome table vessel made of brass, stainless steel or other metal. (Not all firepots are suitable for cooking. Some are merely decorative and shouldn't be used with food at all. This should be checked at the time of purchase.)

The firepot has two main features: a squat, tapered chimney at the center to hold the charcoal, and a circular moat or basin located halfway down, which surrounds the chimney and holds the bubbling liquid. The moat measures about 12 to 15 inches in diameter. The chimney rises 5 to 7 inches above it. A lid with a hole in the center slips over the chimney to cover the moat.

The chimney consists of two compartments, separated by a grate. The upper one holds the charcoal; the lower, the ashes. The amount of charcoal required for a given firepot depends both on the size of the chimney and on the briquets used. (Enough fuel should be added the first time around since adding more at the table will produce untidy ashes.) Also the room in which the firepot is served should always be well ventilated, as is the case whenever charcoal is used indoors.

The briquets, placed side by side in a heavy, foil-lined pan, may be lit in one of two ways: The pan can be set in a preheated broiler close to the heat source. Or, away from the stove, the briquets can be soaked with a fire starter, then ignited. (This is best done out-of-doors, away from curtains and other flammable materials.) In either case, the charcoal is ready when a grayish-white ash begins to form.

Before the glowing charcoal is transferred to the firepot chimney with tongs, the liquid must already be in the moat. If it isn't, the intense heat of the charcoal will melt the solder that holds the firepot seams together.

The liquid—now chicken stock, rather than water—is usually brought first to a rolling boil on the stove, then transferred to the firepot so it will reach the table bubbling vigorously and the meal can begin at once. (The broth in the firepot must not become so hot, however, that it begins to boil away. Should this occur, all the diners may be asked to dip some cold blanched Chinese cabbage into the firepot at the same time to lower the temperature.)

Although the firepot broth is usually served at the end of the meal, it may be sipped and sampled at any point. To re-

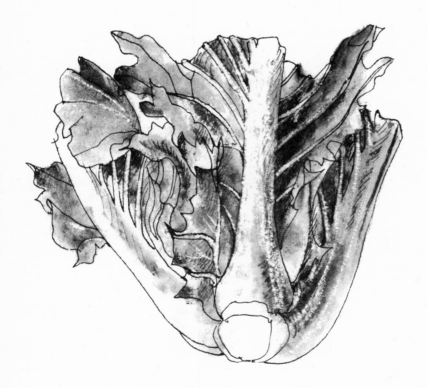

plenish it whenever necessary, one should have on hand another quart or two of stock, which, when added, must also be at the boiling point.

NOTE: The stock needn't be too concentrated to begin with since it will, of course, be further enriched as the meal progresses. It may be prepared by simmering a chicken carcass and giblets in water for about two hours. As they cook, the broth may be enhanced with any of the following, added sparingly: dried Chinese shrimp or scallops (soaked first in wine or water to soften), fresh ginger root, scallion, sherry, light soy sauce, sesame oil, the liquid from canned abalone and salt.

Since the firepot's essential purpose is to keep the liquid simmering throughout the meal, another vessel capable of performing the same function may substitute. It should meet these requirements: hold about 2½ quarts of liquid, be at least 12 inches in diameter and 3 inches deep and keep the broth bubbling at the table. Thus an electric pan of the proper dimensions, set at 250° to 350°F., will do nicely, as will a heatproof casserole or other capacious pan set over a hotplate, small hibachi or adjustable spirit burner.

By way of preparation, raw meat, poultry and fish are carefully trimmed, thinly sliced and cut in uniform pieces—generally in strips ranging from ½ to 1 inch wide and from 2 to 2½ inches long. (The odd-sized scraps, along with the bones, are reserved for stock.) The ingredients are most easily cut if frozen briefly until firm (about 30 minutes in the freezer), then sliced and thawed. Or they can be completely frozen, partially thawed and sliced, then permitted to finish their thawing.

The most suitable beef for the firepot is top round, flank or sirloin steak, sliced diagonally against the grain and cut in strips. Lean pork and lamb are cut in a similar manner, with pork sliced as paper-thin as possible to ensure that it will cook completely. With chicken, only the white meat is used, particularly the breast, which is skinned and boned first, then thinly sliced on the diagonal and cut into strips. Various kinds of liver are suitable: pork, calf, chicken or lamb. After the connective tissue is removed, the liver is also sliced thin and cut in strips.

Any firm-fleshed white-meat fish is fine for the firepot: sea bass, striped bass, halibut, sole, flounder, carp or trout. The fish is skinned and boned; then the fillets are sliced—but not so thin that they might crumble—and cut in bite-sized strips or squares.

Virtually any seafood is suitable: shrimp, washed, shelled and deveined, butterflied if small, cut lengthwise in strips if large; abalone, cut in wafer-thin sticks or squares; raw lobster, shelled, the meat cut in bite-sized cubes; raw crabs, also shelled, their meat picked over for bits of cartilage, and coarsely shredded; small clams, left whole, their shells washed well with a stiff brush (they open quickly in the hot broth); and oysters, shelled first, then cut in half if large.

The flavor of the raw ingredients is sometimes further enhanced by marination. Thus chicken or fish might be tossed gently in a mixture of light soy sauce, sherry and a few drops of sesame oil about 30 minutes before the meal begins. Or shrimp can be sprinkled lightly with sherry about an hour ahead. At the meal itself the diners can flavor their food before cooking by coating it lightly with a mixture of cornstarch, soy sauce and sherry.

Cooking time for all firepot ingredients is brief, the briefest of all for fish and seafood—only a minute or two. Abalone needs so little cooking that it's barely heated through. Liver is also immersed briefly. (It would impart too strong a flavor to the broth otherwise.) Pork requires the longest cooking to lose its pinkness.

Just about any type of noodle can be used: peastarch, egg, rice-flour or wheat-flour. Peastarch noodles—also known as transparent noodles or vermicelli—are particularly favored because of their unique and rapid ability to absorb the subtle flavors of the broth.

Before the noodles are added to the firepot—near the end of the meal—they must first be softened by soaking or parboiling. Peastarch and rice-flour noodles are covered with boiling water for about 30 minutes. Then they're either left whole or cut in more manageable lengths. Egg and wheat-flour noodles are always parboiled in advance.

Once the noodles are added, the firepot is covered with its lid for a minute or two so they can complete their cooking. After the noodles are served, the vegetables are added a handful at a time so they won't reduce the temperature of the broth abruptly. They too are simmered covered a minute or two—until softened but still crunchy.

The most frequently used firepot vegetables are fresh spinach and Chinese cabbage, also called Chinese chard or *bok choy*. The tough stems of the spinach are discarded, and the leaves left whole if small or cut in strips. Only the long white stems of the Chinese cabbage are used. (Their dark green leaves are reserved for heartier soups.) The stems are blanched first, then cut in bite-sized pieces.

Other firepot vegetables include lettuce instead of spinach, bean curd cut in bite-sized cubes, canned or dried mushrooms—the latter softened in hot water first and cut in strips—slivered bamboo shoots, watercress and snow peas.

To season the cooked ingredients, the diner dips them into various condiment sauces. Although such sauces may be prepared in advance, it's customary for each person to create his own at the meal—to work out that combination of flavors that suits his personal preference.

The condiment ingredients that can be combined in any way one chooses include light soy sauce, sherry, vinegar, hoisin and oyster sauce, tomato paste, chili sauce, hot pepper oil, Chinese sesame oil and sesame paste, cornstarch, dry mustard, curry, sugar, salt and pepper. Also any of the following: minced or shredded chives, scallions, garlic, parsley and fresh ginger root.

At a given meal there might be a small dish each of soy sauce, oyster sauce, tomato paste, chili sauce, hot mustard mixed to a paste with water, sesame oil, peanut oil, vinegar, sugar, minced ginger root and garlic, as well as some shredded scallions and Chinese parsley. One might, for example, wish to combine the soy sauce with a few drops of sesame oil; or the chili sauce with either soy sauce or mustard paste or both; or the oyster sauce with peanut oil. Or one might mix to taste the soy sauce, vinegar, minced ginger root and scallion or mix the vinegar, tomato paste, sugar, salt and pepper along with minced ginger root and garlic.

Raw eggs also have a role to play in the firepot. Before the diner dips the cooked food into his condiment dish, he may dip it first in some beaten egg, thus cooling the morsel and giving it a velvety texture as well. Or, after the noodles and vegetables have been served, the diner may poach a fresh egg in the still-simmering broth to finish up the meal. (He can either break it into a shallow plate and slide it into the liquid or else break it into a soup ladle or cupped vegetable leaf and lower it gently into the broth.

Ideally, the table on which the firepot sits should have a heatproof surface. If it doesn't, an asbestos pad can serve as protection. The firepot is then surrounded by the serving plates of the cut-up raw ingredients, with the food decoratively arranged in a single layer, overlapping slightly, fish-scale fashion. (This also makes it easier to pick up.)

The food may be set out on several large platters or more conveniently on a number of smaller ones. (Some of the ingredients can be covered with plastic wrap and refrigerated until needed if they're to be prepared in advance or if the table is small.) The condiments for the dips meanwhile are distributed around the table in small saucers. The noodles, vegetables and eggs—still in their shells—are set out in separate bowls and brought to the table at the end of the meal.

Each diner is given a dinner plate (or a salad plate if the table is small), a bowl for soup, a soup spoon and a dish for mixing his condiments. (The soup bowl is often used for this purpose as well. When the stock is ladled out at the end, a tablespoon or two of the sauce left in the bowl will make the broth more flavorful still.) In addition, the diner receives a pair of chopsticks (sometimes two pairs: one for cooking, one for eating). If chopsticks aren't used, any of the following may substitute: small wire mesh strainers, slotted spoons or long forks with heatproof handles.

Recipes for firepot cooking are versatile, flexible and can be varied at will. For a hearty meal one should allow per person about ½ pound of food and 1½ cups of stock. Otherwise just about anything goes. The following recipes will serve about eight.

THE PEKING FIREPOT

8 to 10 *dried black Chinese mushrooms*	¼ *pound Virginia ham*
¼ *pound vermicelli*	½ *pound fish fillet*
10 to 12 *cups chicken stock*	1 *dozen small clams*
½ *pound lean beef*	½ *pound fresh shrimp*
½ *pound lean pork*	2 *cakes fresh bean curd*
1 *chicken breast*	1 *pound Chinese cabbage*
½ *pound chicken livers*	½ *pound spinach*
	6 to 8 *eggs*

1. Separately soak the mushrooms and vermicelli in hot water to cover until softened (about 30 minutes).
2. Cut up the various ingredients as described previously

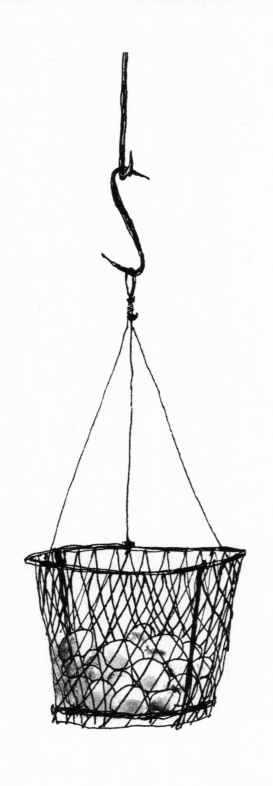

and arrange on serving dishes. Prepare the vegetables. Set the table. Put out a selection of condiments.

3. Bring the stock almost to a boil. Meanwhile ignite the charcoal. Transfer stock to the firepot, then add glowing charcoal to the chimney.

4. Bring the firepot to the table. When the guests have cooked, seasoned and eaten their food, add the vermicelli, then the vegetables. Simmer, covered, a few minutes and serve. Poach the eggs and serve.

5. Ladle out the rich broth as the final course.

MONGOLIAN HOTPOT

1 *leg of lamb*	1 *pound Chinese cabbage*
½ *pound wheat-flour noodles*	½ *pound fresh spinach*

1. Have the lamb boned. (There should be 3 to 4 pounds of boneless meat.) Have the bone divided into manageable sections.

2. Place lamb bones in water to cover. Bring to a boil. Cover pan, reduce heat to low and simmer about 2 hours, skimming broth at intervals to clear.

3. Parboil the noodles to soften slightly. Keep warm.

4. Slice lamb and prepare the vegetables as previously described.

5. Ignite the charcoal. Set the table. Put out a selection of

condiments. Transfer lamb broth to the firepot, then add glowing charcoal to the chimney.

6. Bring firepot to the table. When the guests have cooked, seasoned and eaten their lamb, add parboiled noodles. Simmer covered a few minutes to heat through and serve. Add vegetables. Simmer them covered a few minutes and serve.

7. Ladle out the rich lamb broth as the final course.

NOTE: 10 to 12 cups of chicken stock may substitute for the lamb broth.

FUKIEN FIREPOT

¼ *pound rice-stick noodles*	1 *pound fresh scallops*
1 *dozen oysters*	1 *pound canned abalone*
1 *pound raw shrimp*	1 *pound fish fillets*
1 *bunch watercress*	½ *pound fresh crabmeat*
1 *large bamboo shoot*	10 *to* 12 *cups chicken stock*

1. Soak the rice-stick noodles in hot water to soften. Shuck the oysters; shell the shrimp.

2. Remove tough stems of the watercress and cut into manageable lengths. (Refrigerate until ready to use.) Cut up and prepare the remaining ingredients as previously described.

3. Bring the stock almost to a boil. Meanwhile ignite the charcoal. Transfer hot stock to the firepot, then add glowing charcoal to the chimney.

4. Bring firepot to the table. When the guests have cooked, seasoned and eaten their food, add softened noodles to broth. Simmer, covered, a few minutes and serve. Then add watercress. Simmer about a minute and serve.

5. Ladle out the rich broth as a final course.

PURE STEWING

Pure stewing, another delicate form of Chinese simmering, is used with whole fish and poultry and large cuts of pork. (It's also described as white cooking since it doesn't use soy sauce, as red cooking does.) The ingredients here are immersed in boiling water and slowly simmered until tender in a heavy, covered pot. The clear broth produced is characterized by the ingredient's natural flavors. To preserve this, subtle —rather than aromatic—seasonings are used. These include: fresh ginger root, small amounts of such dried ingredients as shrimp, scallops, lily buds, mushrooms or tangerine peel.

During the last half hour of cooking, fresh vegetables, particularly the root variety—carrots and turnips—may be added along with salt and wine. Sometimes the ingredients are simmered plain, then marinated in wine for an extended period as is the case with Drunken Pork.

Usually the meat and broth appear at the same meal—the soup served in a large tureen; the white-cooked tender meat sliced and presented separately, either hot or cold. Plum sauce, soy-mustard, soy-vinegar or other similar dips are often provided to complement the blandness of the meat or poultry.

WHOLE CHICKEN IN SOUP

1 *chicken (4 pounds)*	1 *tablespoon sherry*
Boiling water to cover	*Salt to taste*
8 *cups cold water*	2 *tablespoons sherry*
1 *scallion stalk*	1 *tablespoon soy sauce*
2 *slices fresh ginger root*	*Few drops sesame oil*

1. Wipe the chicken with dampened paper toweling. Place in a deep pot. Pour boiling water over to cover. Cook 2 to 3 minutes over high heat. Drain, discarding the liquid. Rinse bird immediately under cold running water.

2. Wash pan. Bring the fresh water to a boil in a kettle. Return chicken to pot. Pour boiling water over and bring to a boil again. Add the scallion and ginger root. Cover pan, reduce heat to low and simmer until chicken is tender (about 1½ hours). Season to taste during the last few minutes of cooking with the first quantity of sherry and the salt.

3. Serve the broth in a tureen and the bird on a platter, accompanying it with a dip made by blending the remaining sherry, soy sauce and sesame oil.

NOTE: The chicken should be tender enough to be served whole and eaten with chopsticks, but it may also be carved Western style.

DRUNKEN PORK

1 pork shoulder (3 to 4
    pounds)
1 scallion

2 slices fresh ginger root
Boiling water to cover
2½ teaspoons salt

Medium-dry sherry

1. Have the pork shoulder boned and tied. Place in a heavy pot along with the scallion and ginger root.

2. Pour the boiling water over. Bring to a boil again over medium-high heat. Then cover pot, reduce heat and simmer 30 minutes.

3. Add the salt and simmer covered 30 minutes more. Drain meat and let cool. (The salty liquid can be reserved and combined with an unseasoned stock for later use.)

4. Cut pork in chunks so it will fit into a large jar or crock. Dry meat with paper toweling and put in the jar.

5. Pour the sherry over to cover meat completely. Then close jar tightly and refrigerate 5 days. Drain, reserving sherry for other cooking purposes. Slice meat thin and serve.

SOUPS

The starting point for most Chinese soups—which are generally light and delicate—is a stock made with both chicken and pork. The soup is often sipped throughout the meal, particularly when tea is not served until the very end.

BASIC CHICKEN STOCK

1 chicken (about 4 pounds)   8 to 10 cups water
½ pound pork   ½ teaspoon salt

1. Put the chicken—either whole or cut up—in a pot with the pork and cold water. Bring to a boil over moderate heat, then skim the surface of the liquid to clear.
2. Cover pot, reduce heat to low and simmer about 1½ hours if bird is left whole or about an hour if cut up. Add the salt during the last few minutes of cooking.
3. Cool and strain the stock. Then refrigerate and remove the fat when it congeals.
NOTE: Reserve the meat and poultry for use in other dishes.

EGG DROP SOUP

2 to 3 eggs   1 tablespoon medium-dry
1 scallion   sherry
6 cups chicken stock   ½ teaspoon salt

1. Beat the eggs well. Mince the scallion. Meanwhile heat the stock in a saucepan.
2. Add the eggs to stock, pouring them in a thin stream and stirring constantly. (They will set in narrow ribbonlike shapes.)
3. Stir in the sherry and salt. Sprinkle with minced scallions and serve at once.

SOUP WITH SPINACH

¼ pound lean pork   2 cups fresh spinach
1 tablespoon medium-dry   6 cups chicken stock
   sherry   ½ teaspoon salt
             Dash of soy sauce

1. Cut the pork in thin strips. Place in a bowl. Add the sherry and toss to coat. Let stand about 15 minutes, turning meat a few times.

2. Stem, wash and drain the spinach. Cut the leaves in strips.

3. Place pork and the stock in a saucepan. Bring to a boil.

4. Cover pan, reduce heat and simmer about 20 minutes. (The pork must be completely cooked through and no longer pinkish.)

5. Add the salt and spinach and cook, uncovered, only until spinach begins to wilt and turn bright green. Stir in the soy sauce and serve.

FISH AND LETTUCE SOUP

½ pound thin fish fillets
Lettuce
2 tablespoons medium-dry
  sherry
1 tablespoon oil
½ teaspoon soy sauce
6 cups chicken stock
½ teaspoon salt
Dash of pepper

1. Cut the fish in bite-sized strips or squares. Place in a bowl. Shred the lettuce.

2. In a cup, combine the sherry, oil and soy sauce. Pour over fish, tossing to coat. Let stand about 15 minutes, turning a few times. Transfer fish to individual soup bowls.

3. Bring the stock to a boil and pour it immediately over fish strips. Let stand about a minute. Then season with the salt and pepper, garnish with lettuce strips and serve.

CRABMEAT AND VINEGAR SOUP

1 can cooked crabmeat
2 slices fresh ginger root
1 large or 2 small tomatoes
6 to 8 cups chicken stock
2 tablespoons oil
½ teaspoon salt
2 tablespoons medium-dry
  sherry
1½ tablespoons vinegar
½ teaspoon salt

1. Pick over the crabmeat, discarding any bits of cartilage, then chop coarsely or shred. Mince the ginger root.

2. Plunge the tomato into boiling water for 20 seconds.

Peel immediately, then cube. Meanwhile, in another sauce-pan. heat the stock.

3. Heat a wok or skillet. Add the oil and heat. Add the first quantity of salt and the ginger root. Stir-fry a few times, then add crabmeat, stir-frying gently to heat through and blend flavors.

4. Add crabmeat mixture to stock and simmer, covered, 15 minutes. Add tomatoes only to heat through.

5. Stir in the sherry, vinegar and remaining salt and blend well. Serve at once.

RICE AND CONGEE

Simmering is the way the Chinese cook rice, although the rice, in effect, is as much steamed as it is simmered.

When rice is simmered in a greater quantity of water, it becomes a creamy, souplike congee. This soft, bland, delicate dish lends itself to countless variations with all sorts of ingredients.

Congee, for example, may be accompanied by pungently flavored foods. Or it can be poured over tender raw ingredients and will cook them quickly because its heat-retaining properties make it even hotter than boiling water. Or else various ingredients such as meat, poultry, fish, preserved fruit and sweetened soybeans can be cooked directly in the congee.

Any variety of rice may be used—long grain, oval grain or

glutinous—also millet and barley. Any liquid may be used—water, chicken broth, pork broth, etc. Although cooked rice with enough liquid added can also be simmered to become a congee, raw rice is preferable. Its grains, being more absorbent, produce a creamier smoothness overall. Using a rotary beater after cooking produces a creamier texture still.

Congee is virtually an all-purpose dish: At breakfast 'it's a warming, refreshing hot cereal; at lunch, a thick, nourishing soup; at supper, a filling, satisfying main dish; at midnight, a highly digestible snack.

Basic rice calls for about 1½ times as much water as raw rice. Congee, on the other hand, calls for a ratio of 12 to 15 parts liquid to one part rice. Thus, in basic rice two cups of rice and three cups of water will serve six to eight. In congee one cup of rice and three quarts of water will serve a similar number.

Congee can be prepared in quantity and reheated, with more liquid added if necessary. It can also be frozen and will keep for months. It has been called the magic extender because 12 people can be fed with two cups of raw rice, 1½ pounds of meat and six quarts of water.

BASIC RICE

2 cups long-grain rice   *3 cups cold water*

1. Put the rice in a sieve and wash in several changes of water to remove the surface starch.

2. Transfer rice to a pan deep enough and tall enough to let it expand to more than twice its volume. Add the cold water. Let stand covered about 10 minutes.

3. Bring rice, still covered, to a boil over high heat. When the pan lid begins to jiggle, uncover pot immediately and reduce heat to medium.

4. Let rice cook, uncovered, 2 minutes. (Most of its excess water will then boil away.)

5. Replace lid, reduce heat to very low and cook rice another 18 minutes. Turn off heat, but do not uncover pot. Let

stand 10 minutes more for rice to complete its cooking—then serve.

NOTE: The pan should be made of a metal which conducts heat evenly, such as a heavy-duty aluminum, enamel-clad steel or tin-lined copper.

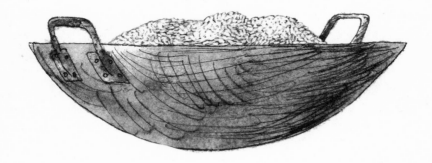

BASIC CONGEE

1 cup rice   *3 quarts cold water*

1. Place the rice in a sieve. Wash in cold running water to remove the surface starch. Drain and transfer to a large thick-bottomed pan.

2. Add the cold water. Bring to a boil uncovered. Then lower heat to medium and cook 15 minutes.

3. Cover pan and reduce heat to very low. Simmer slowly for 2 hours or until the rice grains lose their shape and the mixture takes on the consistency of a thin pudding. Check at half-hour intervals, stirring the congee. (If the mixture seems too thick, stir in more boiling water.)

4. Serve, garnished with shredded or minced scallions, parsley, fresh ginger root or garlic in any combination.

Basic congee can be enlivened during simmering by a slice or two of fresh ginger root, a piece of dried tangerine peel or some dried shrimp or scallops and a teaspoon or two of

peanut oil. During the last five minutes of cooking, a bit of chopped pickled cabbage or a tablespoon of sherry or brandy can be added. At the very end a beaten egg, a few drops of light soy sauce and sesame oil can be stirred in.

While the congee simmers on the stove, various foods can be cooked directly in it, including spareribs, sliced pork, pork liver, chicken and chicken livers, ground pork or beef, roast pork, roast duck, fish fillets (sole, pike, sea bass, etc.), salted fish, fresh shrimp, oysters, clams, crabs, lobsters, abalone, squid, eggs and various vegetables.

Cooking time for each will vary according to its inherent toughness or tenderness and how it is cut up. Thus, chopped meat, slivered lean steak, already roasted pork squares or strips of fish or fresh seafood need only a few minutes each, while fresh pork spareribs, chopped into bite-sized sections, need 15 minutes or more.

When plain congee is to be poured over thinly sliced raw ingredients, they're usually marinated first for about 30 minutes in a mixture of soy sauce, sherry, minced ginger root, sugar and salt along with cornstarch or beaten egg, then transferred to their own serving bowls. The congee, brought to a vigorous boil, is then ladled over. After only a minute or two, the raw food is cooked and ready to eat.

CHICKEN CONGEE

1 *frying chicken (2½ pounds)*	*½ teaspoon salt*
5 *cups cold water*	*½ cup rice*
2 *scallions*	*Dash of soy sauce*
2 *to 3 slices fresh ginger root*	*½ teaspoon ginger root*
2 *tablespoons sherry*	*Salt and pepper*

1. Wipe the chicken with dampened paper toweling, then divide lengthwise in half. Put in a heavy pan with the water, scallions and ginger root. Bring to a boil. Cover pan, reduce heat to low and simmer 20 minutes.

2. Add the sherry and salt. Simmer covered 20 minutes more. Meanwhile wash the rice in cold running water to remove some of the surface starch.

3. Remove chicken from pan and set aside. Add rice to the broth and simmer slowly, about 2 hours, or until creamy and smooth in consistency. (Add more boiling water during cooking if necessary.)

4. Meanwhile bone and dice the cooked chicken; mince the remaining ginger root.

5. When congee is ready, stir in the chicken cubes only to reheat, along with the soy sauce and ginger root. Season to taste with the remaining salt and pepper and serve.

PORK CONGEE

1 *cup rice*	1 *teaspoon sherry*
3 *quarts cold water*	1 *teaspoon soy sauce*
½ teaspoon ginger root	*½ teaspoon oil*
1 *scallion stalk*	*¼ teaspoon sugar*
½ pound ground pork	*Pinch of salt*
Dash of pepper	

1. Prepare basic congee with the rice and water.

2. Mince the ginger root and scallion and combine in a bowl with the pork, sherry, soy sauce, oil, sugar, salt and pepper. Blend well together.

3. Stir the pork mixture into the simmering congee. Cover and cook over low heat until pork is no longer pink (about 5 minutes). Serve hot.

FISH CONGEE

1 *cup rice*	2 *teaspoons oil*
3 *quarts cold water*	¼ *teaspoon sugar*
½ *pound fish fillet*	*Dash of soy sauce*
1 *slice fresh ginger root*	*Dash of white pepper*
1 *tablespoon sherry*	*Parsley*

1. Prepare basic congee with the rice and water.

2. Cut the fish in bite-sized strips or squares. Shred the ginger root and combine in a bowl with the sherry, oil, sugar, soy sauce and pepper, blending well.

3. Pour mixture over fish strips and toss gently a few times. Let stand about 5 minutes. Transfer fish to individual soup bowls.

4. Pour the hot congee over. Let stand about 2 minutes. Mince the parsley. Sprinkle it over each bowl as a garnish and serve.

Congee is also a fine catch-all for leftovers. One can add stock or water to cooked rice—or even to the hard crust that sometimes forms at the bottom of the rice pan—along with leftover gravies, bits of meat or poultry, chicken or pork bones, minced ginger root, scallions, garlic, bits of fresh, dried or canned vegetables, etc. After the mixture simmers gently on the stove an hour or more, it becomes a thick, rich, savory soup.

Ingredient Information

SOME RECIPES IN this book do call for special ingredients, but in most cases, substitutes are possible. If not, the ingredient should be omitted altogether.

Bamboo shoots are the crisp, tender, young shoots of an oriental plant. Sold in cans, they must be rinsed briefly before using. Shredded coarse-textured crunchy vegetables, such as carrots, celery or young turnips may substitute.

Bean curd is a bland-tasting, custardlike product made with soybeans and formed into rectangular cakes about 3 inches square and 1 inch thick. They're sold fresh, dehydrated and in cans.

Bean sprouts, the delicate sprouts of mung peas, which are best fresh, are also available in cans. If the latter is used, the sprouts should be drained several hours in advance, rinsed thoroughly, then immersed in fresh cold water and refrigerated. Thinly sliced celery, shredded young cabbage or string beans—parboiled and shredded—may substitute.

Chinese cabbage is a vegetable with long milky-white stalks and dark-green crinkly leaves. Young celery or cabbage may substitute.

Chinese sausage is made with savory spiced pork and comes in narrow red and white links about 6 inches long. Smoked ham may substitute.

Fermented black beans are small, preserved, strong, salty and pungent soybeans used as a seasoning, usually with garlic. More soy sauce and/or salt may substitute.

Five Spices is a combination of spices consisting of ground anise, cinnamon, clove, fennel and ginger. Allspice or cinnamon may substitute.

Garlic, a member of the onion family, is always used fresh— never powdered. To crush it: place the side of a heavy knife blade over an unpeeled clove. Press down on the knife blade with the palm of the hand gently but firmly so the garlic splits slightly but still remains intact. Then peel.

Ginger root is the thick, fibrous, irregularly shaped root of a tropical plant. Preserved ginger with the sweet syrup washed off may substitute, but never ground ginger; its taste is too different. A slice should be about an inch in diameter and ⅛ inch in thickness. To extract the juice: squeeze a slice or two in a garlic press. To crush: use the same method as for garlic.

Glutinous rice is a short-grained, opaque, somewhat sticky rice which becomes translucent and pearllike when cooked.

Hoisin sauce is a thick, sweet, spicy, reddish-brown condiment made with soybeans, hot peppers, garlic and spices. It's sold in cans.

Mushrooms (dried black) are brownish-black fungi imported from the Orient, with large caps and a meaty flavor. Fresh or canned mushrooms may substitute.

Oil for Chinese cooking can be any clear, bland vegetable oil except olive oil, which imparts too strong a taste and burns quickly. Peanut oil is most preferred for its flavor.

Oyster sauce is a thick, dark, grayish-brown, velvety seasoning, prepared by cooking oysters in soy sauce. It's sold in bottles and cans.

Plum sauce is a sweet, thick, piquant condiment made with plums, sugar, vinegar, chili peppers and other fruits and spices. Chutney mixed with applesauce may substitute.

Salt eggs are duck eggs soaked in brine, which add taste and tang to certain bland dishes. Chicken eggs with more salt added may substitute.

Sesame oil is a rich, amber-colored seasoning with a strong nutty flavor, extracted from toasted sesame seeds and imported from the Orient. Domestic varieties lack its concentrated taste.

Star anise is a small, dry, reddish-brown seed cluster, shaped like an 8-pointed star, which imparts a licoricelike flavor to red-cooked dishes. Anise seed may substitute.

Snow peas are a crisp, green delicate vegetable—used primarily as a garnish—and eaten pod and all. (Before cooking, the tips are snapped off and the strings removed.) Frozen snow peas or parboiled green peas may substitute.

Vermicelli are thin translucent bean threads, made from mung-pea flour, which quickly absorb the flavors of the ingredients they're cooked with. Any thin, delicate noodle may substitute.

Water chestnuts are the aquatic bulbs of an Asian marsh plant, about the size of a walnut, with dark purplish skins. The peeled, canned variety should be rinsed briefly before use. Cubed raw celery, sometimes crisp apple cubes, may substitute.

SUITABLE CUTS OF MEAT

Beef

For stir-frying: flank steak or round steak
For braising and stewing: chuck steak, eyeround or beef shin

Pork

For stir-frying: lean boneless meat from fresh pork shoulder,
butt, loin or pork chops
For braising and stewing: chuck steak, eyeround or beef shin
ham
For deep-frying: the same cuts as for braising
For steaming and also for pork balls: the same cuts as for
braising, minced or ground

INDEX

Gloria Bley Miller is also the author of *The Thousand Recipe Chinese Cookbook,* called "the most authoritative and comprehensive" work on the subject. This book was featured on the Today show and won the Tastemaker Award as best cookbook of the year.